HAMMOND'S®

CANDIES

History Handmade in Denver

MARY "CORKY"
TREACY THOMPSON

AMERICAN PALATE

Published by American Palate
A Division of The History Press
Charleston, SC 29403
www.historypress.net

First published 2014

Manufactured in the United States

ISBN 978.1.62619.716.9

Library of Congress Control Number: 2014952361

Notice: The information in this book is true and complete to the best of our knowledge. It is offered without guarantee on the part of the author or The History Press. The author and The History Press disclaim all liability in connection with the use of this book.

The soul is dyed the color of its thoughts. Think only on those things that are in line with your principles and can bear the light of day. The content of your character is your choice. Day by day, what you do is who you become. Your integrity is your destiny—it is the light that guides your way.
—Heraclitus

In memory of Carl T. Hammond Sr. and Carl T. Hammond Jr., whose lives epitomized this philosophy
In honor of Carl T. Hammond III, who shared their stories

Contents

Acknowledgements

There is an apprehension inherent in attempting to thank all the individuals who have contributed to any book, but it is worse still not to make the effort; I owe a debt of gratitude to all those who guided me in my research and opened up the wonderful world of candy making.

To Bill Hansen, Denver attorney and amateur local historian and author, I owe tremendous thanks for his invaluable list of resources and research possibilities. Not only did he jog my memory about available tools, but, incredibly, he supplied me with the actual newspaper citations that he had unearthed in the digital collection at the Denver Public Library: Western History and Genealogy. He also loaned me several books from his personal collection that proved invaluable to me as I broadened my knowledge of the history of Denver and, in particular, North Denver, where the history of the Hammond's Candy Company took place.

Special thanks, also, to the staff at the Denver Public Library: Western History and Genealogy for their diligence in assisting me with additional sources of information and for their patience in introducing me to the idiosyncrasies of microfiche. I want to thank staff members at History Colorado for introducing me to information in the *Colorado Yearbooks* and my daughter, Julia Thompson, for providing news accounts from current media.

Anna Abromowich, sales and marketing coordinator at Hammond's Candies, was unfailing in her prompt responses to my e-mail inquiries and her assistance in setting up appointments and introducing me to Hammond's personnel. Kammy Stucker, production manager, helped plan my kitchen tours and photo shoots, and I owe thanks to Ginny Gleason, Melissa Joslin and Jane Powell for their continual welcome at Hammond's tour office. Mickey Theuambounmy graciously shared her experiences of thirty-two years as a Hammond employee.

I am grateful to Ralph Nafzinger, who shared his insight into the transition that Hammond's Candy Company made as it evolved from a family-owned company through its first outside ownership to its current structure. His knowledge of past and present production and sales, as well the culture of the different phases of the company, was most helpful in preparing this manuscript. Of course, none of this would have been possible if Andrew Schuman, CEO of Hammond's Candies, hadn't generously welcomed me and shared his goals.

My thanks in preparing this manuscript also go to Becky LeJeune, commissioning editor at The History Press, for her guidance, encouragement and professional recommendations; to Michael Scalisi for his many contributions to the color photo section; and to Lloyd Rich for his advice.

Most important in the writing of this book, however, was the opportunity to hear the stories of the Hammond family, to learn its values, to understand how its members persevered and succeeded and maintained their company. I came to know and admire Carl and Laura and Tom and June and their children and grandchildren. For that I thank George Hammond for taking the time to visit with me. To Emery A. Dorsey IV, Robin Hammond's husband, I am indebted for opening the wonderful world of the confectionary art, as well as his family stories.

This book, however, would never have been written without Carl T. Hammond III. From the time that I first contacted him, Carl has been unfailing in his information about the family history, his knowledge of the industry and his understanding of the relationships that were the underpinning of the Hammond's Candy Company. I cannot thank him sufficiently for his interest and willingness to explain processes (and to correct my misconceptions) and for enhancing these pages with descriptive, enlightening and often amusing anecdotes about the family members. I thank him, as well, for loaning his photographs and for his willingness to edit, correct and improve this manuscript.

To everyone, then, to all those individuals who generously spent time with me to bring the story of Hammond's Candies to life—thank you, this is your book!

Chapter 1

School's Out

Grandpa Peach

Denver mornings start with a dry, cool and invigorating temperature, which makes it easy to look forward to the day, but Carl Hammond didn't have great expectations when he awoke at the crack of dawn on that late summer Monday. Today would be his first day of high school, and he wasn't one bit excited. In fact, he had very mixed feelings at the thought because he had already decided that what he had learned in elementary school was all the education he needed for the time being. He knew his older brother Harry didn't agree with him, but despite the encouraging words of his brother, Carl felt four more years at school would be useless. He realized it was important for him to earn some money if he wanted to enjoy more than the room and board and bare essentials that his father would provide.

Harry, two years older and already aware of the courses he would need if he went into the construction business, felt no such qualms. But he understood that the prospect of sitting in a classroom at North High School bored Carl, who was anxious to find his way in the workaday world. Like an elder brother, however, he urged Carl to drag himself out of bed, get dressed and set out for school. The iconic North High School had not yet been built on Speer Boulevard, so Carl presented himself that day at Ashland School, which then housed both elementary grades and high school. Ironically, about

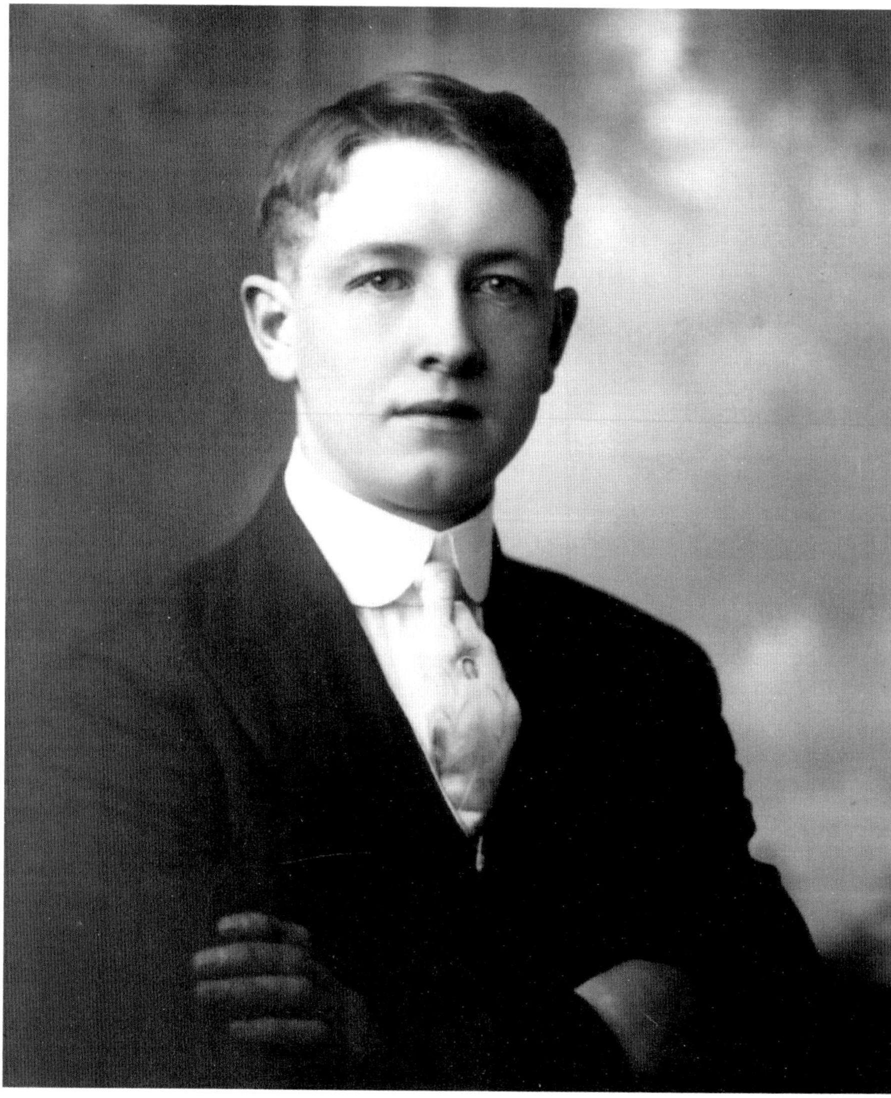

Portrait of Carl Hammond Sr. as a young man. *Carl T. Hammond III Family Collection.*

thirty-five years later, he would build a factory for his Hammond Candy Company directly across the street. But Carl's early opinions turned out to be well founded, so when he got home that afternoon, he announced that he didn't need any more education. "Fine," his mother replied, "but you're not going to lie around the house. Go get a job."

And that's just what Carl Hammond did—he got a job as an apprentice for the Cosner Candy Company on Welton Street.[1]

Independence was a trait he had inherited from both his parents and his grandmother as well. She had become a widow at a young age, but that situation wasn't unusual on the plains, where accidents claimed many lives and some men were felled just by the exhaustion of tilling the soil. It was hard, hard work running a wheat farm successfully enough to provide for a family of five sons and, hopefully, put something aside to provide for old age. It was harder still for a young woman who now had all the household chores and the vegetable garden to manage, but it was possible for someone like her who took pride in her resilience. She was undoubtedly aware that with her brood she wouldn't seem very attractive to the bachelor farmers in the area, and she might easily not have found the thought of another marriage very appealing. Instead, she hitched up her buckboard and drove into town to the feed store, where she had enough credit to purchase sufficient seed for the next year's crop. At a time when a weaker woman might have been tempted to pull up her roots and return to her family, or move to another place for easier opportunities, or just give up entirely, Carl's grandmother persevered, raising her sons until they were grown. When Carl's father, Thomas Hammond, known as Peach, felt the pull of independence and announced his intention of looking for greater opportunities in California, she let him go. If the prospects of the uninhabited land offered by the Homestead Act of 1862 had lured the family to Lawrence, Kansas—where Peach was born on August 9, 1867—perhaps the growth of the state's population prompted Peach to think of trying his chances elsewhere. There had only been 107,206 people living in Kansas in 1860, and by 1880 that number had exploded to 996,096.[2] It was a Hammond characteristic to seek personal, if not necessarily physical, space for growth, and with four other brothers living on the farm, perhaps Peach felt that was getting a bit crowded, too.

At any rate, Peach's mother gave him, as she did all her sons, the very generous sum of $2,000. With the same dogged determination that had enabled her to conquer the vicissitudes of weather on the prairie, she had overcome the trials of single parenthood and, over the years, had frugally squirreled away about $10,000 from the sale of the wheat. Today, her gift would equal a little less than $50,000, a healthy start in life for any young man.[3] When for family reasons Peach decided that California was too far from Kansas, he stopped in Denver and made it his home. Peach, too, handed down to Carl the kind of flexibility and hardiness that had been his mother's legacy to him.

Peach and his wife, Mary, whose family hailed from Pennsylvania, separated after they moved to Colorado, although they never divorced. Peach then left Denver and homesteaded in Oak Creek, Colorado, where he lived off the land, raising cattle and occupying a two-room shack of about three hundred square feet. Many years later, Peach's grandson Tom's wife, June, nicknamed the cabin the "most painted shack in Colorado." It seemed that whenever her friends from her Masonic group, the Daughters-of-the-Nile, needed to get away for just a little peace and quiet, they would visit the shack and paint it. The activity was probably a good justification for leaving everything behind for a day or two.

The town of Oak Creek is situated in the rich and fertile Yampa Valley in Routt County, just south of Steamboat Springs. Periodically, Peach would slaughter a steer, load the carcass onto a buckboard and then drive it over 150 miles to Denver, where he would sell the meat from his wagon at the side of the road. In the warmer months, the trip was arduous, traveling over the Gore Pass, which, at an elevation of 9,524 feet, was approximately 2,000 feet higher than Oak Creek. In winter, the journey was brutal, if not downright forbidding, but that didn't deter Peach's resolve to navigate the rough trails. He would take the wheels off his conveyance and add runners to handle the snow, which in some places could exceed several feet. The drifts, caused by the howling wind, increased the hazards for both Peach and his horse, which had to be fed and sheltered from the elements before Peach could get any rest. What today is about a three-hour drive in good weather, and frequently considered to be hazardous in snowy conditions, would have taken four days and nights for Peach. When it came time to sleep, he wrapped himself in blankets and hunkered down under the buckboard.

As he got older—he lived to be ninety and died on October 29, 1957—and was no longer able to continue these exploits, he spent time at Carl's candy factory, sweeping the floor or helping with odd chores, because he was the kind of man who had to have something to do. That Peach truly characterized the hardy pioneer spirit is reflected in a story recounted by one of his great-grandsons. By that time, Peach was living in a nursing facility, where his son Carl would visit on Sundays. When asked on one occasion what he had done to his hand, Peach's reply was that nothing had happened, totally ignoring the fact that his hand was wrapped in a much bloodied handkerchief. Upon further investigation, Carl discovered that Peach had closed a window on his finger, cutting it off up to the first knuckle. That was just another example of the hardy independence that typified Carl Hammond's heritage.

Sweet Prospects

Carl was born to Peach and Mary on November 21, 1895, in North Denver, a part of the city that until shortly after the depression of 1893 had been the independent town of Highlands. "True to her name and nature," the town's report for 1891 reads, "she stands high and sightly, where the pure air from the mountains—that God-given slayer of disease—is first-hand by her people and sells their lungs with strength and healthfulness. [There are] no smelters, factories or emitters of smoke within her borders."[4] In addition to his older brother Harry, he had two younger sisters: Doris, born two years after him, and Mabel, three years later.

Carl must have gained a variety of experiences as well as a love of the candy business during those initial years of employment, since in 1911 he listed his occupation as driver and, later in 1912 and 1913, as teamster in the Denver City Directory. However, Cosner's would prove to be a good choice, for the confectionary business was booming and was considered to be an industry with great growth potential. As early as 1882, Milton Hershey's father, who had come to Colorado from the East with an early tubercular condition, had encouraged his son to move to Denver, a city he considered to be fertile ground for entrepreneurs. Following his advice, Milton moved west and found work with a local candy maker. While employed by this confectioner, whose name has been lost, Hershey learned an important process for making candy that held the key to his future success. The Denver confectioner taught Hershey how to make caramels with fresh milk, which not only enhanced its flavor but also gave it an important chewing quality that eastern candy makers were then achieving with the use of paraffin. Armed with this new formula, he soon left Denver to seek out opportunities in Chicago and New Orleans and ultimately returned to his native Pennsylvania, where he proceeded to make his name known.[5]

Although little is known about those first few years that Carl spent in the candy industry, he had been fortunate in finding employment with one of the top confectioners in his field. E.M. Cosner was a respected businessman who recognized the advantages the Colorado climate offered. He noted in an article he later wrote for a local business journal that marshmallows made in the East will dry and crack if shipped to high altitude and, if dipped in chocolate there, will splinter when shipped to this climate.[6] An early twentieth-century issue of the trade magazine *Candy and Ice Cream* carried an article that proved Mr. Cosner's point about marshmallows. Its headline read: "4 Tons Candy Seized and Owners Fined in Court. Marshmallows

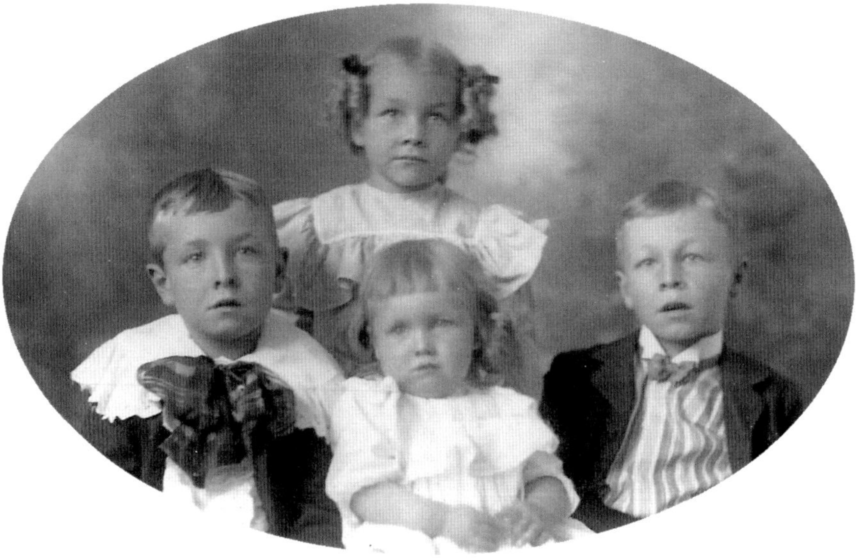

Carl Hammond Sr. with his three siblings: Doris (top), Harry (far right) and Mabel. *Carl T. Hammond III Family Collection.*

That You Can Hammer Are Shown to Judge. Denver, Co." It seemed that a Mr. A. Lang, a wholesale jobber at 1221 Nineteenth Street, declared that he was willing to eat a pound of candy every day for a year from a batch of four tons that he had bought recently in Salina, Kansas. The shipment had been condemned by the city and federal health officials as units for sale. Lang made his extraordinary offer in municipal court before Magistrate Stapleton, but his offer was turned down, and he was fined $100 and costs after the health officials had pounded marshmallows and chocolate fudge with hammers to demonstrate to the court that it would make better building material than confection.[7]

Mr. Cosner also stated that chocolate cream centers will not hold up in Colorado's climate if made in a low altitude, and since he believed that disease germs do not exist in a high, dry area, he added that candy manufactured in Denver's air, which is light, dry and pure, was healthier than that made at lower altitudes.[8] Whether this claim was true at the time, his assertion helped to ensure the success of his enterprise.

W.C. Nevin, whose company bore his name, also shared Cosner's belief in the importance of Colorado's high altitude, writing in the same article that because of the humidity in the East, pillows and glossy cuts (very popular hard candies to this day) must be enclosed in glass or hermetically sealed. He added that chocolate had to be artificially refrigerated, thereby excluding fresh air from the product.[9] Clearly, it was a popular conviction that the industry Carl Hammond was joining not only gave pleasure to people but also added to their general well-being.

Off to War

Unfortunately, like so many young men of his generation, Carl had to interrupt his early career in 1917 when he was drafted into the army when the United States entered World War I. He served in France with the Rainbow Division in the field of communications. Responsible for carrying telephone wires on his back through the lines—often a hazardous duty in the event of enemy fire—he was decorated for his service before his discharge.

Similar to most of his compatriots in this and later wars, he spoke little of his front-line experiences, but akin to many of his noncommissioned peers, he did enjoy telling a few stories at the expense of his commissioned superiors. A favorite, according to a family member, recounted a march through exceedingly muddy fields, a trek that the troops thought the officer ordered for the sake of showing his power. Unfortunately, the new captain neglected to call the order to halt in a timely fashion, and the first two ranks fell into a very wet trench.

Carl only once spoke very briefly of a horrific incident in the trenches when a shell exploded, killing two soldiers, one on each side of him, and leaving him completely untouched. In relating this story to his grandson, Carl III, he simply remarked, "How does that happen?" He made much the same comment regarding an almost mysterious incident that also occurred while he was in France. The troops were frequently poorly supplied with even the most basic necessities, and for men who were constantly on the move, the lack of adequate boots was a critical condition. When the soles wore out, which was often, their only solution was to use whatever material was available as a substitute. Since this was usually cardboard, the solution was short-lived. (This shortage was also the common cause of a disease aptly called "trench foot," which, if left untreated, can, in the worst cases, lead to gangrene and ultimate amputation.) One night, while Carl and some comrades were grousing with soldiers from another company in a local café about their cold, miserable feet, a stranger who overheard them intervened with welcome news. "Oh, I can get you some boots," he said. "What size do you want?"

"Eleven C," Carl responded and handed over the money the other man requested. Later that afternoon, he walked to the appointed street address to get his new boots, only to find out there was no such address, just an empty open field. He felt foolish and ashamed to have trusted a total stranger. He waited in vain for the stranger to appear. Discouraged, he set off across the open field to return to his quarters, and as he waded through the muck and debris, he stumbled over something blocking his path. Looking down, he discovered a pair of boots, miraculously size 11C. "How does that happen?" he again asked. Carl, who had a laconic nature, didn't really expect a reply to these queries.

He grimaced a bit, but with a twinkle in his eye, at the memory of the unsavory conditions on the crowded troop ship crossing the Atlantic. Sleeping on the stacked bunks sometimes presented difficulties, but it was the sanitary facilities that made even the more hardened men balk. The majority of the soldiers on board, especially those from cities and the more urban areas of the country, enjoyed indoor plumbing at home. Even those used to outdoor latrines were startled to find that they had to use open troughs, filled with running water pumped in from the ocean, that spanned the width of the vessel. When the ship encountered the heavy seas characteristic of the Atlantic, it helped to have nimble feet to escape the inevitable sloshing.

BRECHT'S MAKES LIFE SWEETER

At the end of what for a time came to be called the Great War, Carl returned home, anxious to resume his career, and soon apprenticed at the Brecht Candy Company. G.A. Von Brecht, who was described in the *Rocky Mountain News* as a capitalist from St. Louis, had established his company in 1915, after his purchase of the defunct Austin Candy Company. Von Brecht proposed to invest the lordly sum of $100,000 to modernize the Austin facility at Fourteenth Street and Wazee to make, in his words, the "new factory one of the largest and best in the country and certainly the biggest west of the Mississippi river [*sic*]."[10] The building still stands at that location, but while the sign "Home of Brecht's Chocolate and Candies" has long been replaced to advertise its latest tenant, the slogan painted on the Speer Boulevard side of the building remains: "Brecht's Candies—Makes Life Sweeter."

Von Brecht had rushed his plan to install the latest and best machinery for the manufacture of candy, and although he had announced his proposal in the middle of October, he had his factory up and running by November 15, just in time to supply the Christmas trade. His company was a boon to the North Denver economy since it employed approximately two hundred people, eighty more than the Austin Company had hired.[11] At that time, Mr. Brecht had no reason to know that he would probably lose most of those men to the war that the United States would enter two years later.

It is probable, therefore, that Carl Hammond was one of the many whom Brecht needed to hire when the war ended and a workforce was once more available. Carl had good company and good opportunities while at Brecht. He recounted that on lunch break, he and his buddies used to go up to the roof to smoke. While there, they would watch the horse-drawn wagons straining to scale the viaduct with their loads and try to guess which horses could reach the top, still moving upright, rather than staggering under the weight they were carrying. Like the teams he was watching, Carl worked diligently, rapidly learning the intricacies of making the hard candy that was Brecht's specialty and honing an innate business sense. His bosses were attuned to the skills he displayed, promoting him to production manager in the short time he worked at Brecht.

Although there is no record of Carl's salary while at Brecht, the average annual wage in the 1910s was approximately $750 (which translates to a mere $11,800 in 2014), and in the 1920s, this had only increased to $1,236 (or $14,650). It is no surprise, therefore, that with Carl Hammond's entrepreneurial spirit and the skills he learned while at Brecht, he soon decided to strike out more or less on his own.[12]

Unfortunately, there is very little history about Carl's earliest endeavors in the Hammond family annals. What is known is that in about 1922, Carl began working for his brother Harry Hammond, who, true to his ambitions, had gone into construction as he had planned when he decided on the necessity of a high school diploma. In the 1923 Corbett and Ballinger's directory, in which Harry's address is given as 2339 15th Street, he is listed as a carpenter. He owned his own business, building single detached homes (one at a time), industrial buildings and renovations. Carl worked for Harry during the day and made candy at night behind a small storefront located at 1411 Platte Street. Eventually, Carl spent more time making candy than working construction. By the time the city directory of 1920 was published, he was listing his occupation as candy maker.

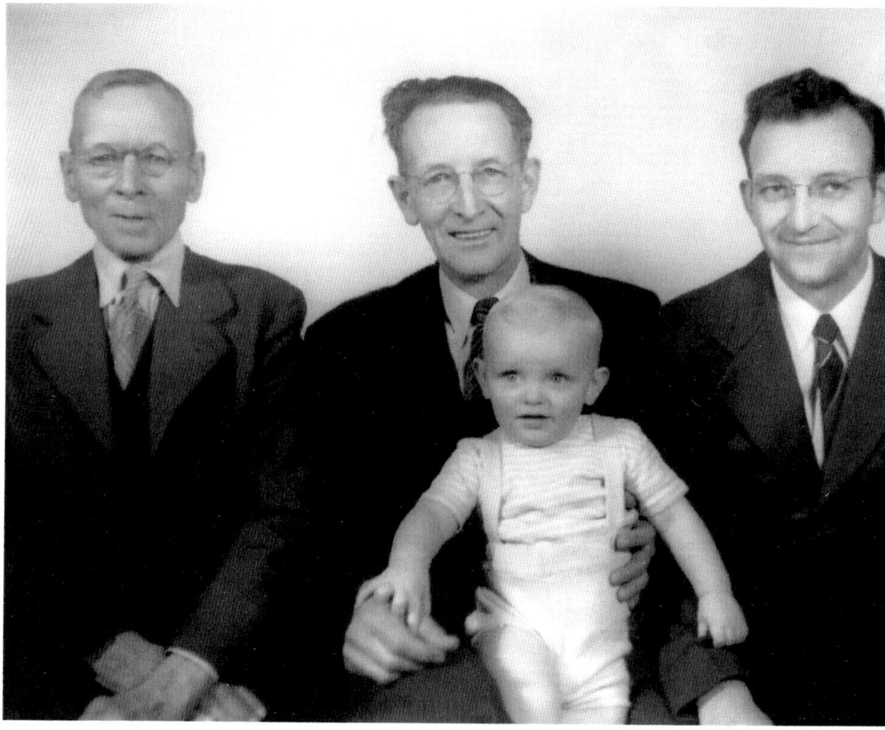

Four generations of the Hammond family: Peach, Carl Sr., Carl Jr. (Tom) and Carl III. *Carl T. Hammond III Family Collection.*

This, then, is the story of how Carl Hammond created a small family-run business that sustained itself through a depression, the Second World War and the onslaught of crushing competition from domineering global conglomerates and, with the founder's passing, continued on to the next generation. It is the unique history of a company that has emerged with the same handmade products that are faithfully produced, often using the same machinery, as they were one hundred years earlier.

Chapter 2

A Career for Life

Wedding March

The year 1920 was a banner one for Carl T. Hammond. On August 2 of that year, he married Laura L. Johnson, the only child of a family from Capitol Hill, which many considered in those days, to be a long way—socially, if not geographically—from North Denver. Carl's grandchildren don't know how the two met, but it was probably not a union the Johnsons would have chosen for their daughter. They had come to Colorado from Philadelphia and chosen to live in an affluent community where they spent freely from their inherited money with no other visible signs of support. They undoubtedly enjoyed the society of bankers, lawyers and old Denver merchants rather than that of shopkeepers and factory workers. Like many of their neighbors, they lost their fortune during the Great Depression. Since Carl and Laura Hammond were both Christian Scientists, at least in name, this church affiliation might have been the bridge that spanned their economic divide.

There were two or three Johnson sisters and a brother, and as time went on, they all adjusted to having a relative in "trade." Carl's grandsons remember being invited to spend the night, and sometimes the two clans shared holiday celebrations. A favorite family story evolved from a Thanksgiving dinner in the early 1950s when Laura's Aunt Mary had been invited.

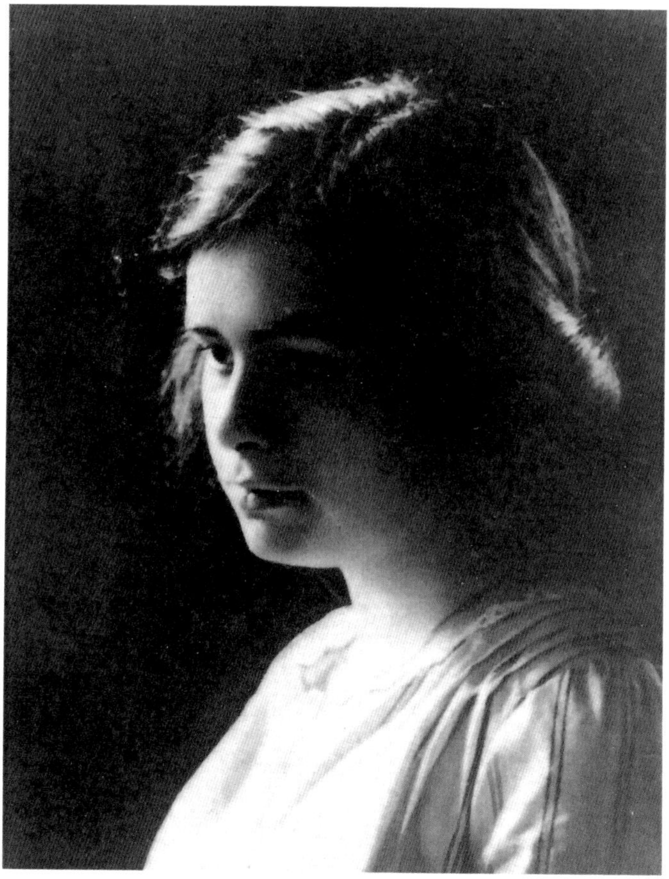

Left: Laura Johnson Hammond at the age of sixteen. *Carl T. Hammond III Family Collection.*

Opposite: Carl Sr. and Laura with their first grandson, Carl III, in the garden on Newton Street. *Carl T. Hammond III Family Collection.*

Carl had a wonderful sense of humor, despite his pragmatic nature, but on this day he was in particularly rare form as he presided at his table and looked down at the large number—about eighteen—of family members gathered for the feast. Aunt Mary, who was over seventy, was very hard of hearing. She tended to talk loudly, and she could hear others as long as she was looking at them. Like many elderly people who won't admit to needing a hearing aid, she was probably reading their lips. Eight adults would sit at a long table, while Carl presided at the head of the table, carving the turkey onto plates, which were then passed down the table to his guests. This was the first year that Carl III, the eldest grandchild, was big enough to sit at the grown-up table, so he remembers this story well.

While Carl was cutting the turkey, Aunt Mary kept asking over and over, "Why don't we have goose? We have turkey every year. I think goose

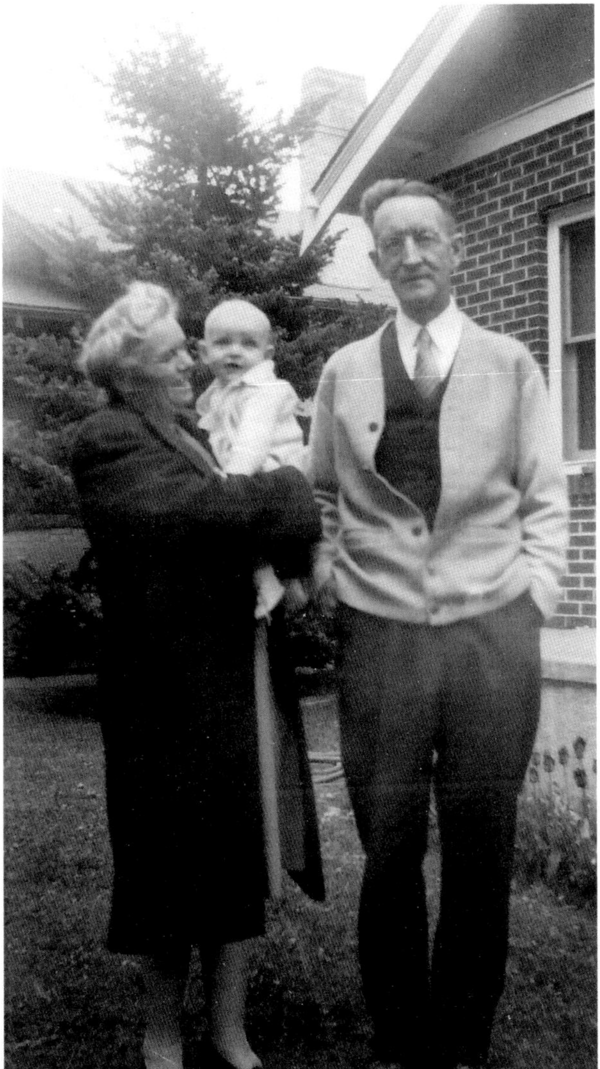

would be nice. I don't understand why we can't have goose. Why don't we have goose?"

Carl, with his eyes on the turkey, quietly replied, "If you get me a broomstick, I'll give her a goose."

This was greeted with a roar of laughter except from Aunt Mary, who chirped, "What'd he say? I couldn't hear him. What'd he say? What'd he say?"

No one replied; they were laughing too hard. Carl III was laughing too, but he was too young to know what was so funny. To many of Carl's associates, this would have been a new glimpse of the man.

Whatever the social differences there might have been, Carl and Laura's marriage would endure for a lifetime and into the next generations, and it proved to be a partnership that flourished through both business and family life. This was also about the time that Carl bit the bullet and left Brecht. That, too, was the start of a lifetime proposition, for he would never again work for another man or another company and would remain proud of his status as a small businessman for the rest of his life.

Denver Good Times

The year 1920 was also a good one for anyone with youth and vigor and creativity and a healthy desire to work. Denver was a thriving city, open to new ideas and anyone who wanted to act on them. Agriculture and ranching were quickly taking the place of mining, and farmers and others employed in the mountains and plains depended on the city, which remained a center for distribution and transportation. But the people also looked to Denver to fill their cultural needs and provide recreation and entertainment.

In 1896, a citizen gave the mayor of Denver a black bear cub that had come to City Park, and at that moment, the Denver Zoo was born. However, it gained true stature and interest with the 1918 opening of Bear Mountain, which was the first institution in the United States to feature animals living in their natural setting. It was a revolutionary idea that is still a beloved attraction at the zoo.[13] Equally popular and at first showcasing the collections of naturalist Edwin Carter, the Museum of Natural History (now the Denver Museum of Nature and Science) attracted families as well as scholars. It, too, was located in City Park, making it easy for people to walk between the two facilities.

In downtown Denver, the Municipal Auditorium had opened in 1908, in time for the Democratic National Convention, and it was not only the largest building of its type west of the Mississippi but was actually second in size nationally only to Madison Square Garden in New York City. Its planners and architects had chosen its design with forethought. With its movable proscenium, its seating capacity ranged from 3,326 to 12,000, depending on how its proscenium was arranged. It was possible to stage concerts, operas or plays, but it was also possible to offer basketball games or even a national convention.[14] Summer theater was a favorite way to end a day at Elitch Gardens, an amusement park that debuted in 1890, when Mary and John Elitch turned their farm on the outskirts of the city into an oasis for urban residents. By 1920, its Trocadero Ballroom featured top bands of the day and offered a chance to dance or just enjoy the music. During the 1990s, Hammond's Candies operated a retail outlet at Elitch's near the Trocadero Ballroom.[15]

Denver was clearly not a city in the center of the country, but it was central to a large area around it and offered something for almost everyone.

A listing in the 1923 edition of the Corbett and Ballinger directory records that Laura and Carl Hammond resided at 2103 Clay Street and included an additional notation of Walton and Hammond. It might be presumed with the order of the names that Walton put up the capital for this business, although there is very little history about this first endeavor in the Hammond family annals. Many years later, in 1977, an article in the *Denver Post* quoted Carl Jr. in describing Clendon S. Walton as a bookkeeper.[16] A picture does exist of a windmill-shaped building labeled "Walton and Hammond Ice Cream Factory, 1932," but this date must have alluded to the time the sketch was made, since the partners had severed their relationship long before that year.

"It was not a successful business," Carl once told his grandson and namesake, Carl III. Like many entrepreneurial first attempts, it was a lot of work for very little money. "At the end of the day," he confided again to the same grandson, who was still in junior high school, "I looked in the till, and there was nothing there. I decided that was no way to live, so I closed the business up."

From that time on, he was truly his own man and his own boss.

"Business Conditions Good" announced a headline in the *Rocky Mountain News*, citing the experience of J.X. Kennelly, advertising manager of the Goodyear Tire and Rubber Company, as he traveled throughout the western states. It was almost as if he was writing the primer for Carl Hammond's first foray into business as he cited the example of two tire dealers he called on in the same town. The first was wailing about the dire conditions of business as he sat in his office, complaining that unless things picked up, he would have to find another location. He hadn't sold one tire that day. On the other side of town, the second dealer had no time to talk to Kennelly because, recognizing the demand for his product, he had promoted it forcefully and had already sold thirty-two tires since opening in the morning."[17] The newspaper quoted Kennelly further, "Aggressive salesmanship…can usually be depended on to increase sales."

FIRST FACTORY

Whether Carl ever read that article isn't pertinent, since he already knew the importance of location and established his first candy factory where there would be plenty of foot traffic and access to a buying public. The North Side Commercial Association had been busily promoting the area for several years.[18] Small manufacturers and retailers of all kinds filled the surrounding streets, including the Schwayder family's luggage shop, which later gained fame as Samsonite.[19] Across the street, a grocery store and a saloon promised

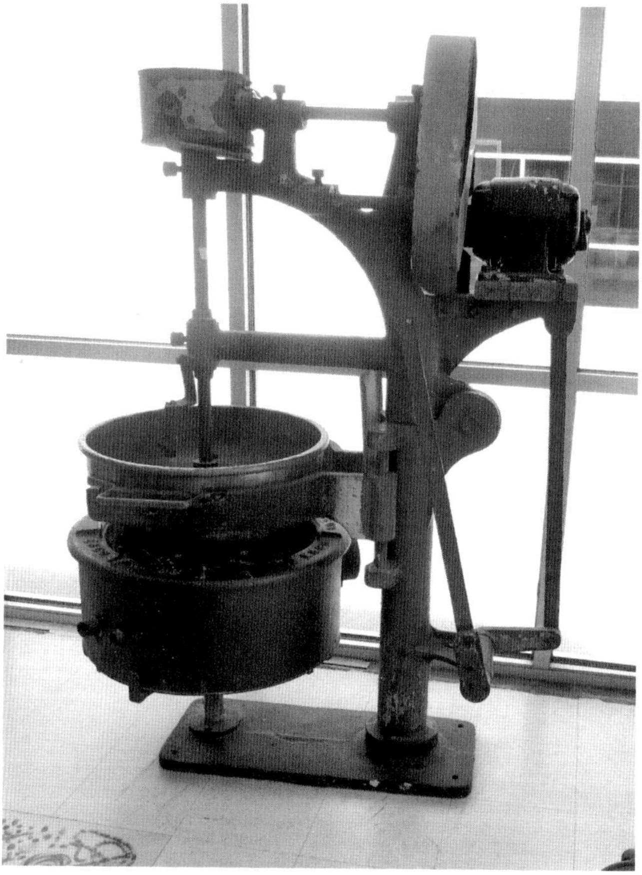

The old fire mixer, used by Carl Sr. in his first factory during the 1930s, is now in the tour office. *Photo by the author.*

additional patrons, possibly those over-imbibing husbands who might assuage their wives with a guilt offering of a bag of sweets. Fifteenth and Platte is still a busy corner, although the site now serves as the parking lot for REI across the street.

Among the many pitfalls that could entrap novice candy makers were the regulations required by the Pure Food and Drug Act, which became law in 1906 and was amended twice before Carl entered the confectionary market. Of particular concern to him would have been the provisions regarding color additives, a popular method used for increasing eye appeal for candies. Throughout the history of mankind, one can find examples of adulteration of foods or misleading claims, and as early as the middle ages, bakers were fined for adding chalk to their dough to achieve a brighter white appearance. In the fourteenth century, French dairy farmers were prohibited from adding color to butter (reminiscent of the margarine wars centuries later), and as late as the 1880s, a study in Boston found that 46 percent of candy sampled contained at least one toxic mineral pigment. Horrifyingly, it was predominantly lead, and during the nineteenth century, almost all food contained some kind of contaminant. Some people even refused to drink milk, since much of it had been tinged with lead chromate that colored it with a yellowish cast, artificially making it appear richer and creamier and more like its actual counterpart. All that was changed by the federal law of 1906, but in 1899, the National Confectioners' Association had already advised its members to discontinue use of twenty-one specific color additives. Advances in chemistry, which had alerted the manufacturers as well as the buying public to the dangers of many food additives, had also underlined the greater possibilities of liability and prosecution in the case of adulterated foods. The act specifically forbade the use of colors or stains that might conceal inferior or damaged products.[20]

But the Pure Food and Drug Act covered much more than what a manufacturer intentionally added to his products, as one unwary Denverite learned to his dismay when he was unexpectedly visited by a state pure food commissioner. The news report described the premises of the Curtis Street candy man as "filthy, full of cats and excrescence of every description." He was arrested and later pleaded not guilty. It should be noted that this transgression took precedence over the variety of assaults, larcenies and burglaries listed in the same news article.[21]

Advertising, although prevalent in the popular magazines and newspapers of the time, reached many fewer citizens before the advent of the radio, so wily merchandisers tried a variety of maneuvers to lure consumers into their shops. One ploy, apparently popular from New York to the West Coast, was the use of the candy board, which some likened to a form of gambling. The basic form was simply a board containing a number of paper-covered holes. Players would pay for the opportunity to punch open a hole in the board, behind which was a small numbered slip. If the numbered slip matched the number printed on the front of the board, then the buyer won whatever prize corresponded with the number. In Denver in 1920, candy punchboards were popular with both store owners and their customers—the former viewed them as an important trade stimulant, and the latter enjoyed them as an inexpensive game of chance. But this was an era that also spawned Prohibition, and the more cautious of citizens sought to have punchboards banned for fear of instilling a love of gambling in children. An agreement between the Western Candy Manufacturers' Association and Mr.

Frank M. Downer, manager of safety and excise, solved this problem with a provision that the boards could not be used in stores within two blocks of any school.[22] This readiness for compromise provided a more comfortable climate for conducting business than existed in other parts of the country such as Jackson, Michigan, where Chief of Police Sam Nunnery instructed his men to arrest anyone who operated candy boards in the future.[23] There was much to learn besides candy making for anyone seeking to make it a profitable career.

But in the long run, candy was just candy, delicious to eat and wonderful to make. Candy was big business for everyone—and profitable as well. It made a wonderful gift; it could be bought on the way home from school; it tasted good. In addition to the favorable climate for making candy, Colorado also offered the ideal conditions for growing its chief ingredient, sugar. There was plenty of irrigation water available, and the soil was rich.

Colorado Sugar Beets

In the early twentieth century, Charles Boettcher and partners recognized this when they founded the Great Western Sugar Company in northeastern Colorado with the first sugar mill in Loveland, Colorado. By 1920, newspaper articles made clear that this had become a thriving industry with an estimated tonnage of 1,738,000 for the ten sugar factories that formed the company. At twelve dollars per ton, that meant prosperity for farmers raising the beet crop, and it also meant jobs for the several hundred men and women who left Denver each fall to take advantage of the seasonal work. Before mechanization arrived to simplify harvesting the crop, Swedish immigrants as well as German-Russians constituted the main labor force in the fields. As early as 1902, Great Western was recruiting workers from the more southern states, as well as Mexico, adding important cultural and societal changes to the state.[24]

To someone unfamiliar with the production of sugar from beets, a *Denver Post* headline that read "Sugar Factories Will Slice Beets"[25] might seem misleading, for this step, which follows the harvest, in no way leads to the food a family might find on its dinner plate. In appearance more elongated than globular like its deep red cousin, production of sugar from this plant is a complicated procedure. Following the slicing step, which reduces the roots to thin chips, the beets are put through an extraction process that produces a sugar solution called juice and then pressed and cleaned through another step called carbonatation; they are then boiled down to form the sugar crystals that are finally ready for commercial distribution. In this way, sugar beets differ greatly from sugar cane, which visitors to a sugar plantation in Central America or just a few southern states can enjoy just by chewing on the cane. In the end, both types of sugar can be used for candy making, just as both are sold for individual consumption. For Colorado confectioners, moreover, the proximity of this local sugar beet industry translated into large cost savings for them since their transportation charges were greatly reduced. It was advantageous to the sugar growers that a byproduct, beet molasses, could also be sold to ranchers for cattle feed or sent to fermentation plants to produce alcohol.

Candy Tips

Carl's tenure at Brecht's Candy had introduced him to the mechanics of his new career, but working for a large company is critically different from becoming the manager who makes all the decisions. Now he controlled the purchasing, manufacturing, accounting and sales, but most important to his success was acquiring the not-so-simple understanding of how to run the trade.

In addition to hands-on learning, there were already a number of trade magazines and manuals, and large confectioners joined the National Confectioners' Association, one of the oldest trade organizations in the world. It is doubtful that the fledgling Hammond Candy Company subscribed to this group, but Carl could easily have read other available materials. Jake Friedman's *Common Sense Candy Teacher* (Express Prepaid ten dollars) guaranteed to make money for you hand over fist, assuring its purchasers that it was as beneficial to business "as a spring tonic to a man." It covered just about every imaginable kind of candy from crystal work to pearled seeds, listed a variety of possible formulae and contained valuable pointers to the employer and workman.[26] Another more reasonably priced handbook costing five dollars—perhaps because it was manually typed rather than printed—was available from Candymakers Supply House in Philadelphia. Entitled *Professional Candy Manufacturing, Formulas and Secrets of Candy Makers*, its opening paragraph stated, "Candy is one of the most staple articles on the market and the candy trade in this country has grown to enormous importance, and as the country increases in size and prosperity the opportunities for making money in the candy business become greater and greater. The reason for this is that candy is bought by old and young, rich and poor, and that it has no seasons, but sells equally well the entire year round." Although the booklet is undated, the directions for a Yellow Jack Bar suggested a selling price of five cents for a two-ounce bar, while the Chop Suey candy recipe was valued at forty cents per pound. Among its most unusual offerings was the method for producing Sauer Kraut candy, but that might have reflected the German heritage found in the Pennsylvania community of its publication. A list of important utensils for the beginner candy maker to own included a large pot, a good-sized spoon and a flat, shallow pan for cooling the candy. The instructions included definitions for the hard and soft ball stages, as well as how to perform a water test. It also warned of the "danger point" at which the confection was close to burning. These last directives were added in the event that the new cook had neglected to buy a candy thermometer, which only the most experienced confectioner could safely ignore. Perhaps the most important advice appeared implicitly in the statement, "The main difficulty with most people in starting a candy business is that they try to make too many different kinds."[27]

Whether Carl ever resorted to a similar trade book, it is interesting to realize that such basic information is about as true today as it was almost one hundred years ago when Hammond's started. Carl certainly overcame the admonition in the book regarding "they try to make too many different kinds" as he developed the unique skills to successfully make and sell over 150 different items, from chocolates to hard candies and everything in between.

Chapter 3

Creating Candy

Kitchen Accounting

Carl created his first original recipe, a fluffy honey and coconut center dipped in coconut and milk chocolate, and named it aptly, Honey Ko Kos, but first he had to adapt the candy-making procedures he had learned at Brecht's to his small operation. Any home cook who has ever attempted to produce fudge or fondant frostings or toffee knows that it is simultaneously a simple, yet risky, process. The basic ingredients of corn syrup, sugar—either beet or cane, although Carl would have used the former—and water don't change, nor does the prime importance of the temperature to which each batch is heated. Failure quickly looms for the unwary who ignore this last fact.

With income and expenses now his sole responsibility rather than just a corporate entry on a balance sheet, Carl had to learn to work quickly and accurately in producing his confections. It was a business that many entered, and they found, to their chagrin, that the rate of failure verged on the astronomical. In 1926, *The Colorado Yearbook* listed seventy-two confectionary and ice cream manufacturers;[28] in 1928, when the yearbook separated the two industries, there were only forty-five confectioners;[29] by 1939–40, that number had tumbled to eighteen.[30] Carl must have seen some of these other entrepreneurs come and go, but from the beginning, he was an astute businessman and avoided the others' mistakes.

Money couldn't have been very plentiful in those early years, but Carl learned to spend his wisely, and it is said that he never bought any equipment new, taking advantage of what became available as others closed their firms. Unbelievable as it may seem, some of what he originally purchased is still found on the factory floor today. In his first few years, Carl did it all: he developed the recipes, made the candy, sold the candy and was his own office staff. For generations of Hammond family candy makers, the original formulae could be found in a small three- by five-inch ring binder that served as the bible for anyone who needed a refresher or was new to the company. "To be a small businessman you always have to make the right decisions—one slip and you are gone," Carl once told a family member. He clearly recognized the relationship between creating a product and its profitability on the open market, and he quickly learned to capitalize on the quality of his candies. If something worked once, it could be counted on for the future. If it didn't, he was not afraid of trying something new.

Carl's first kitchen would have had to contain certain basic necessities. He probably started with an open hearth furnace, about three and a half feet in diameter and standing two feet off the ground. The stove had to be large for the flames to produce the high heat needed to boil the candy syrup, and he would have used a long-handled paddle, about three to four feet, to stir it in a large copper kettle. In a small candy factory like Carl's, ordinary tools that could be purchased at a local hardware were, and still are, the implements of choice to achieve the desired result. When it came to mixing the hot, heavy syrup, axe handles were used since they were the desired length and strength. When the temperature reached around 320 degrees, depending on the type of candy he was making, Carl would have poured it onto a steel table, called a slab, to cool it. Other equipment that he would have needed were three-foot-long, one-inch-square metal bars; a series of large spatulas; one- and two-quart tin measuring pitchers; and round steel bars to flatten the candy as it cooled. The last essential piece that Carl needed was a heavy metal hook, about an inch in diameter, that ended in a point; as candy cooled and became malleable, he would throw it over the hook and pull it down until it was about two feet long. Carl had to keep re-hooking and pulling it down to make it softer and lighter, and he would generally manage this in quantities of twenty or thirty pounds at a time. As a solo practitioner in his small kitchen, Carl spent long, sweaty and hot days at work, and it is important to remember that not only was he the sole candy maker, but he was also the only dishwasher and, like everything else in his kitchen, it was a hand operation. Even today, although there are many

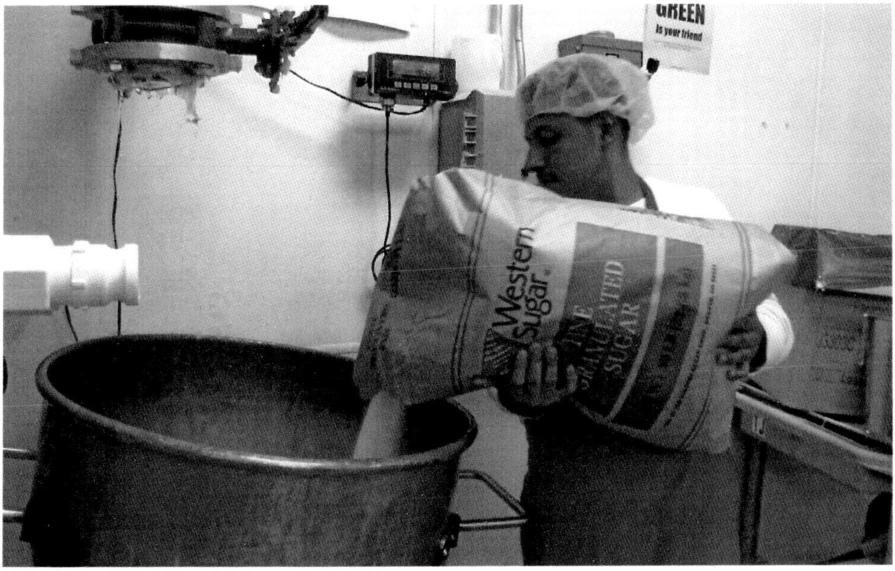

Pouring sugar into the huge cooking pots requires as much brawn today as it did in Carl Sr.'s time. *Photo by the author.*

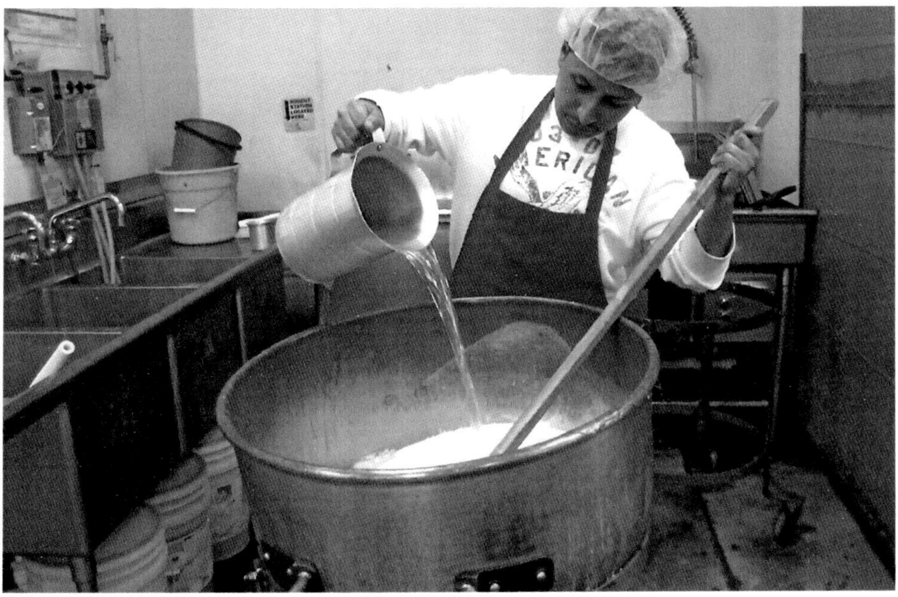

Adding and stirring water into the candy batch is still done using the traditional axe handle. *Photo by the author.*

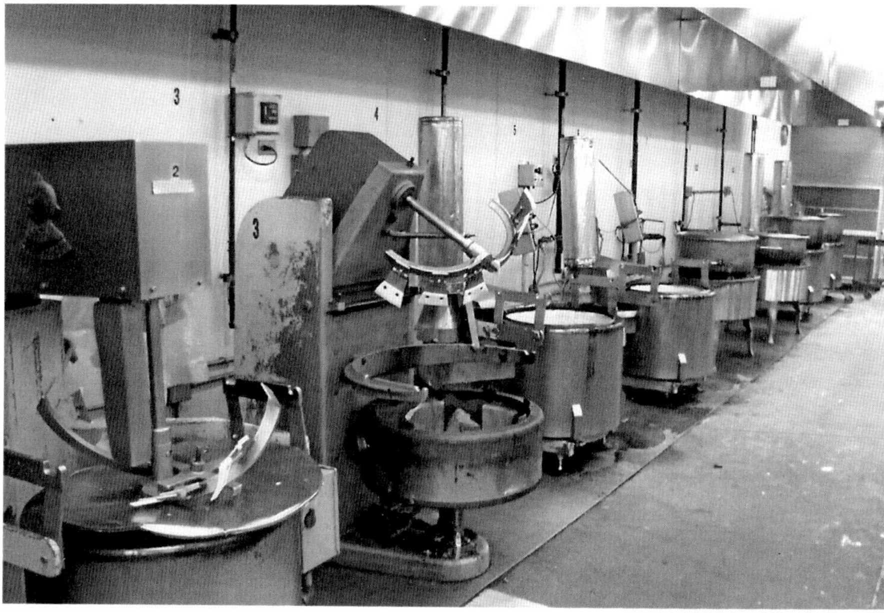

Cooking pots and fire mixers in Hammond's kitchen. *Photo by the author.*

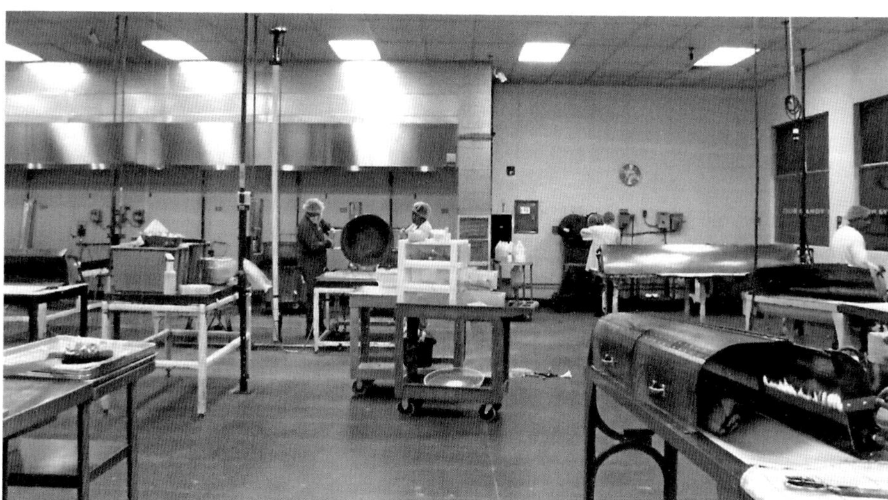

Hammond's Candy kitchen, where all the candy is made; note the menorah loaf in the batch roller at lower right. *Photo by the author.*

workers at Hammond's Candy, a visitor will still see the workers scrubbing the huge copper pots and tables. A more detailed description of how the candy is made is found later in this book, as is a glossary that describes the equipment.

Counting Costs

Clinton H. Scovell, who contributed articles to *Candy and Ice Cream* about the time Carl went into business, cautioned newcomers to the industry, "Do you know your costs?...When candies that sell from five or ten cents a pound up to forty or fifty cents are made in the same department, and often on the same machine, it is absolutely necessary that a reliable method of figuring costs be used to make sure that all these lines are profitable." He continued:

> *Considering the business as a whole I find that candy is made in many comparatively small factories, as well as in the huge plants which are characteristic of other lines of industry. As a natural result, competition is very keen, and some of it not as well informed as it should be, because a man starting in business with small capital has not as much experience as a man who has accumulated and is using the large investment. A second important consideration is that most candy manufacturers are making a great variety of product...Every manufacturer must sooner or later face the problem of having reliable costs on each kind of goods that his factory produces. Much work in the line of accurate cost finding has been done in...many other industries, but as far as I know, nothing similar to the care and accuracy with which these costs are figured has been worked out by the candy manufacturers. The principal difficulty is that the candy business is considered "peculiar" and most practical candy manufacturers have not believed that modern accounting applies to them."*[31]

Unfortunately, he didn't elaborate further on the meaning of the word "peculiar," but his concerns about cost accounting would have been important for the neophyte. Many years later, armed with the accounting skills he had acquired in his accounting classes, Carl III attempted to improve on his grandfather's use of index cards to document his costs. Fortunately, Carl Sr.'s practical experience prevailed over his grandson's less realistic, intellectual approach; small businessmen like Carl don't have time to read it, they have to do it and do it right every time.

Too much could be made of Carl's reluctance to attend high school, since at that time only a small percentage of Americans graduated from secondary schools, and in no way did he denigrate the importance of education. It simply meant that he believed there were alternative ways to achieve learning. According to a grandson, he read *Barron's*, the Dow Jones weekly newspaper widely considered to be the nation's most influential financial journal, every day. While there is no way of knowing when he initiated this practice, it is interesting to note that the two shared a similar longevity, since that venerable magazine started in 1921.[32] Carl always maintained a strong will to succeed and exercised the means to achieve his aims. The fact that Carl built a successful business in the face of all the competition from similar companies that came and went attests to his innate ability to recognize what products should be continued and what should no longer be part of his line. He clearly had an inborn sense of profit and loss, and it could be said that he earned his MBA on the job. The financial shenanigans that led to the great Wall Street crash in 1929 could be found to a much lesser degree in the dealings of small merchants and manufacturers throughout the United States, but never in Carl's business dealings. He never incurred any debt other than regular trade terms. That he never bought anything he didn't have the cash for was one of the pillars of his success. "Debt is death" was his frequently repeated creed.

WHOLESALE EXPANSION

As Carl became established in his neighborhood as a purveyor of fine confections, he expanded into a wholesale business and added at least one employee to free himself to expand his market. He proved to be as good a salesman as he was a confectioner, as shown in another family story. One day, a customer came in to place a wholesale order with a list he had prepared to leave with Carl. As he was about to walk out, satisfied he could get all he needed the next day, Carl stopped him with the question, "Do you have any hard mix? You should really get a couple of boxes." The customer thought it over and agreed that he would like to increase his order and would be back the next day. That buyer probably enjoyed a good night's sleep, but now that Carl had gotten his sale, he stayed up until three o'clock the following morning

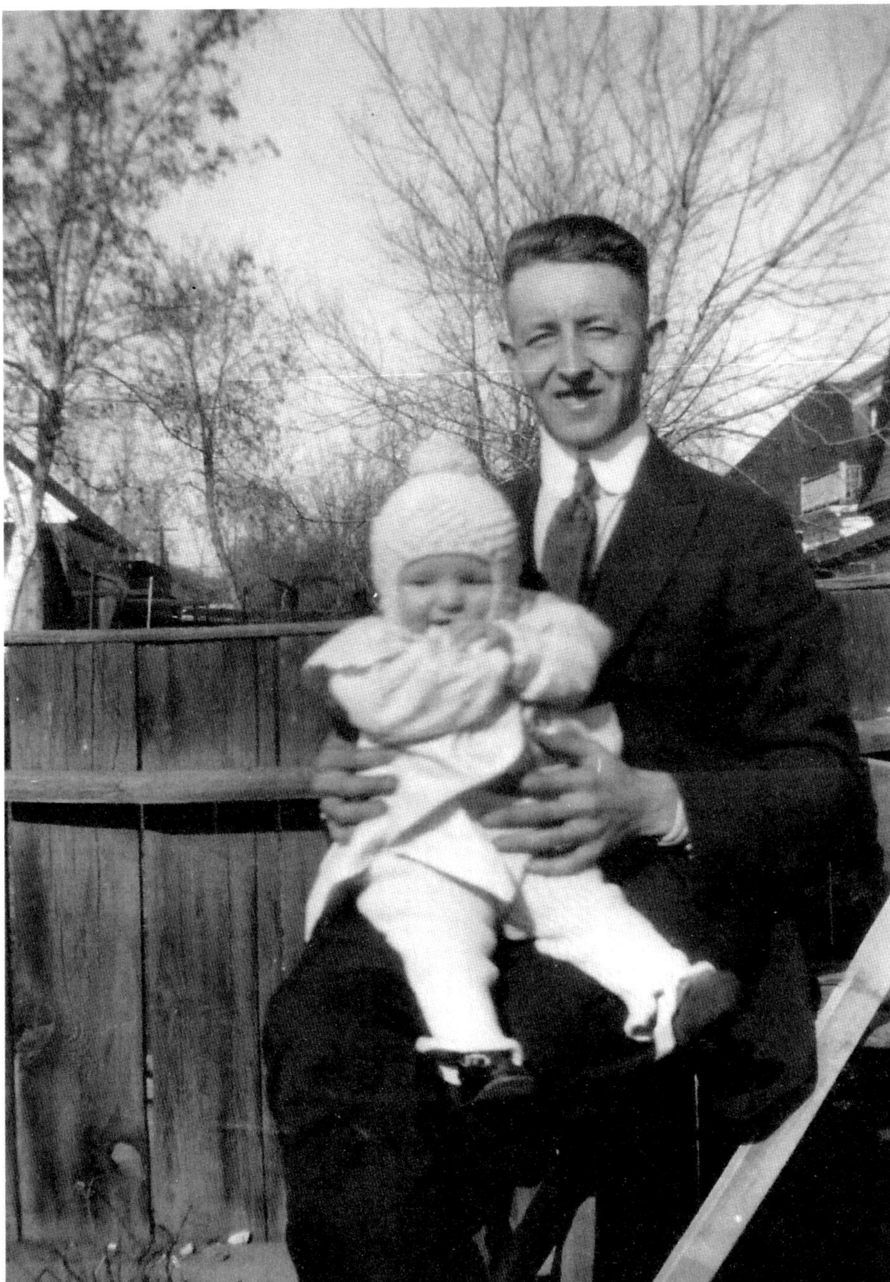

Carl Hammond Sr. shows off his namesake, known as Tom, about 1923. *Carl T. Hammond III Family Collection.*

to get the mix together. In addition to an understanding of how to make his venture successful, he was just never afraid of long hours and hard work.

Although the phrase "24/7" was still a term that wouldn't be used until far into the future, it would have been an appropriate description of Carl's typical day. In addition to his long hours at the shop, he had also become a family man: Carl Thomas "Tom" Hammond Jr. was born in 1922, and Marjorie followed in 1924. That same year, Carl and Laura's address was listed in the annual Denver Householder's Directory at 2103 Clay Street. The house was located on a quiet street, and it had a small front porch that could be blocked to keep Tom and his sister from falling down the steps or running into the street. Even better, it was just a short walk to Jefferson Park, an almost seven-acre area where Laura could bring the children to run around and release their energy, and it was also an ideal spot to meet other mothers and indulge in adult conversation while the youngsters found their own playmates. The Town of Highlands had drained a lake there in 1891, and for a few years after the park was established, the nationally acclaimed Sells-Floto circus used it as its winter quarters.[33] It was a little less than a mile from the house to Carl's factory, a nice walk downhill for his morning commute, but the evening uphill trek must have felt arduous at the end of his long days.

Although every shop offers its own unique specialties, they are really variations on a theme, and candies can be divided into several general categories. Carl would have learned to make all of them as he started out—hard, caramels, chocolates, brittles, fondants and marshmallows. Like all recipes, formulations evolve, and Carl brought basic recipes and techniques from companies he worked with prior to opening Hammond's. From his early success, it is apparent that he had an innate knack for the process since he recognized, as he later explained to one of his grandsons, that "the art of making candy is the art of controlling the crystal in the sugar." Many years later, his son Tom put it another way after he had taken over the business and was explaining the technique: "All you do when you make candy is cool the crystals and then you control the crystallization. Agitation plus heat makes crystallization."[34] Carl also never diverged from his emphasis on the importance of quality methods to maintain the best flavors. A good example of this is still used in the factory today. Water is needed to dissolve the sugar, but once that occurs, its usefulness is ended, and it has to be removed. Hammond's still carefully cooks the water out, while larger competitors and manufacturers of cheaper products use a vacuum procedure to remove it. Carl maintained that his method resulted in a truer flavor.

Candy Center of the West

By 1920, Denver had squeaked onto the list of the twenty-five largest American cities and had reached a population of 256,491.[35] It was considered "the distributing center of the territory lying between the Missouri River and the Pacific coast and the Canadian and Mexican borders."[36] It was a time of economic upheaval but also a period in which the city recognized the importance of supporting its many smaller industries. One of its great successes was the joint exhibit of Denver wholesale confectioners, which the Industrial Bureau of the City and County of Denver sponsored.[37] Hammond's Candies would have been too small to participate in this event, but the fact of the convention emphasized how many purveyors of sweets flourished at that time.

If Carl needed further proof that he had entered the right business, he had only to pick up the October 12, 1923 issue of the *Denver Times* with a headline that heralded "Denver Proving Candy Center of Entire West."[38] The article, which once again touted the climate as being a prime reason for the industry's success, also announced the reactivation of the celebration of Candy Day, a festivity inaugurated by the National Confectioners' Association throughout the country. World War I had interrupted the recognition of the day, but the Colorado Confectioners' organization was joining with the national body in awarding prizes to dealers and retail stores for the best displays of candy in their windows. Encouraging consumption of these sugary treats was certainly the order of the day, but one aspect of the event clearly indicates how attitudes have changed in the past ninety years. E.M. Cosner, the secretary of the association and owner of the company where Carl first whetted his appetite for candy making, announced that he would give a radio talk on the Reynolds broadcasting station to schoolchildren of the state and invite them to submit essays to be used in promotions. The winners would also receive prizes. But the major candy makers did not view youngsters just as unwitting or innocent customers of their products, as witnessed by Jacob Straser, who had opened his plant on Blake Street in 1920. He opined, "Youngsters are far more discriminating in their appreciation of good candy than most people concede."[39] Obviously, candy manufacturers all recognized the importance of the youth market—after all, who is most likely to be seen on the street licking a lollipop or a candy cane? Today's critics might frown on this kind of marketing to children, but most children in the 1920s had much less discretionary income to indulge at the candy store, and there were very few fat children to prompt any such outcry.

Chapter 4

Depression Years

Penny Candy

But the good times of the 1920s—when that old adage that "God helps those who help themselves" proved profitable for so many Americans—came to their crashing end in 1929, and no one was immune to its effects. Bank failures, unemployment, diminishing wages for those lucky enough to have jobs—all contributed to a national malaise. In Denver, the city found that its earlier boast of being a central transportation center came back to haunt it, since it now became an easy and attractive magnet for hobos and transients en route from no place to nowhere. One of the less glorious moments in Colorado history came with the accusations and blame being assigned to Mexican nationals for the economic crisis and the establishment of roadblocks to prevent them from moving freely. The newspapers dubbed that unfortunate policy the "bum blockade." State government often found itself in opposition to edicts emanating from Washington, particularly in response to providing the matching funds mandated by the National Recovery Administration. Unfortunately, one of the ways of raising those monies, since Governor Edwin C. Johnson strongly fought against an income tax, was a sales tax that was levied on a variety of goods that included groceries. This only exacerbated the problems everyone faced in putting food on the table. The governor was so opposed to the New Deal and its Federal Emergency

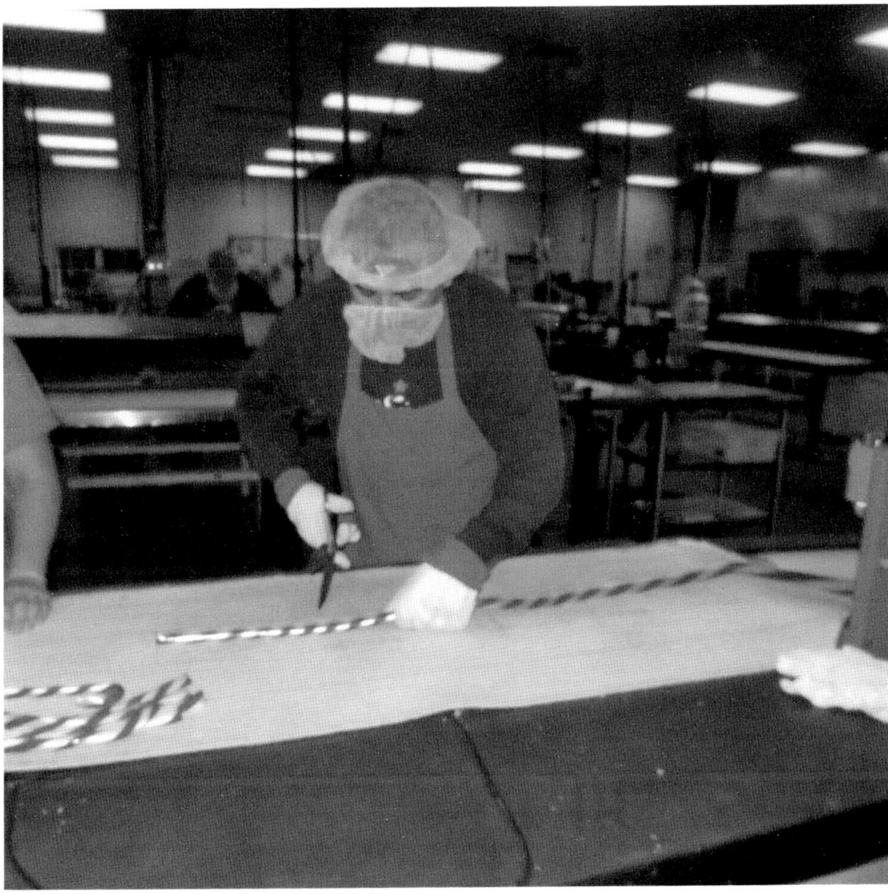

Cutting candy cane lengths before adding the crook. *Photo by the author.*

Relief Administration regulation that states had to raise one dollar for every three they received that he influenced the legislature to refuse to act on raising funds. At one point, the federal aid was actually cut off. Of course, it wasn't the power brokers who were hurt but the householders who had elected them.[40]

Carl faced the dilemmas of the Depression with his usual fortitude and ingenuity, putting his focus on the "penny" candy products. Family lore includes stories of the number of small candy canes he would get out of a single batch. (Today, Hammond's canes are available in much larger sizes, and the variety of flavors has expanded considerably from the original, but the familiar red-and-white peppermint is still the most popular; the canes

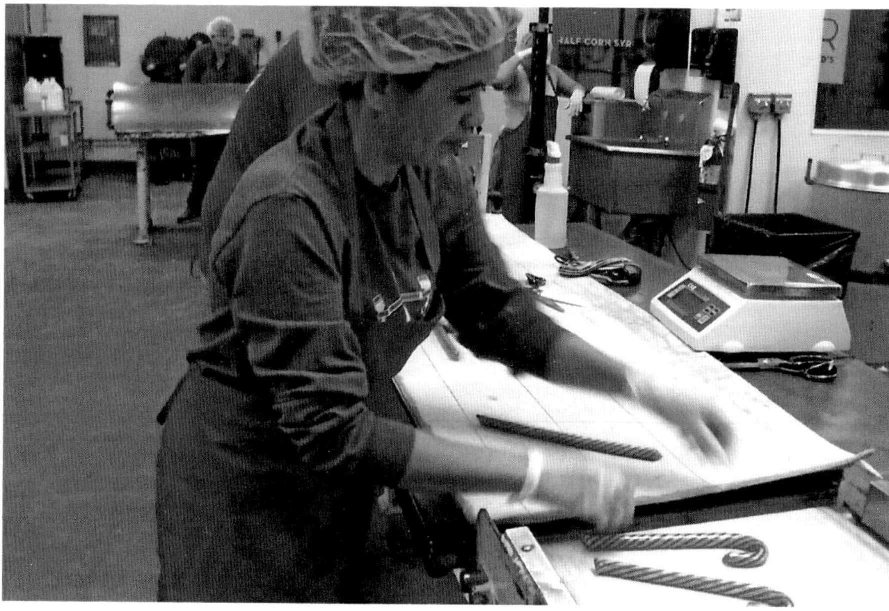

Adding crooks to candy canes. *Photo by the author.*

still rank as the number-one hard candy seller.) Carl recognized that candy could be a solace to people enduring hard times and that if he made it sufficiently inexpensive, they could and would buy it. If people couldn't splurge on buying dinner out, they might treat their family to a small bag of Hammond's sweets. Carl continued to make it all, but he considered hard candies to be his signature product, and he profited from that preference when he needed to market at a low price.

But selling candy in those quantities didn't buy his family's meat and potatoes, so as one answer, Carl hired Bill Hiney, a colleague he knew from Brecht, to make the candy. While Carl then worked for Harry, although construction must have been slow, Laura ran the store and Bill produced the candy. Ginny Gleason, who later ran a candy store in Denver and now greets visitors to Hammond's tours, enjoys her childhood memory of the shop in the 1930s. She remembers Laura looking pretty in her organdy apron, while a helper in a pink dress reached past the curtain at the back of the glass showcase to select her choice. It was usually a difficult decision, choosing either a cream or a caramel.

Emery Dorsey, who later became Tom Hammond's son-in-law and whose family also ran a small business, describes stories of the period:

Those were difficult times—folks were without jobs, and there was virtually a confectionery on every street corner, yet most found ways to sustain themselves. Family became critical to survival, and sons and daughters took their places alongside their parents in the back and front of these small establishments. Walking into a local shop meant being greeted by name, followed by lighthearted inquiries about family and children. Quality and service were the most important considerations of the time. Of the many tales of challenges and hardships, the common thread that tied individuals together was the support of community and the significance of family. Intentions were not set on extravagant amounts of money or even success; it was the conscious efforts to help and to sustain each other that mattered.

In 1931, the Nevin and Brecht candy companies—the former had been founded forty-seven years earlier, and the latter had been a relative newcomer to Denver when Carl and Bill worked for it—announced their amalgamation as one operating organization. The press reported that each would continue to function as a separate entity "with its own staff of executives and with virtually no reductions in working forces." "Greater economy of operation" was the key reason given for the consolidation, so it might be assumed that Bill's job was one of those cut and that he was then available when Carl needed a candy maker for his little factory.[41]

In fact, it must have been galling to have been a struggling entrepreneur like Carl in 1934 when the *Denver Post* headlined in one of its articles that "Rocky Mountain Business Holding Above Last Year," adding in the body of the story that general business conditions were staying above the previous year, despite the slowness with which some goods were moving at retail.[42] Similar optimistic comments were reported at the celebration of the fiftieth anniversary of the Chamber of Commerce,[43] but that could be construed as either blowing in the wind or as an honest effort to convince the public that, despite their personal difficulties, times were improving. Another more tangible effort to bolster the average Denverite's optimism on the state of the city's affairs was the assertion that it was the second capital of the United States. This was based on the number of federal agencies that had major offices or were based in the municipality. The list included the chief reclamation office, the U.S. Bureau of Roads, the Home Owners Loan Association, a new bureau and an internal revenue office that gave employment to more than one hundred individuals.[44] Strangely, the United States Mint—which dated to 1858, shortly after the discovery of gold in Colorado—wasn't even mentioned as an important factor in boosting

Denver's status as one of the country's most important urban regions. It is also paradoxical that the city aimed to be like the nation's capital while the state was busy affirming its state's rights.

#1 Mitchell Sweet

The assets that probably helped Carl the most in surviving the Great Depression were his integrity and his very strong sense of self. He knew that he wanted to provide a good product that people would want to buy and appreciate, and if, at the end of the day he could say he had done that, then he was satisfied. One day, a friend approached him with a delicious confection that he had invented and that he thought Carl should taste. Carl bit into it, a soft, bite-sized marshmallow surrounded by succulent caramel; he loved the product and purchased the recipe to produce in his factory, naming it the "Mitchell Sweet" after his friend. The Mitchell Sweet became a signature candy in the Hammond's line, and today it has been in continual production at Hammond's for almost ninety years. It still ranks number one among the soft candies sold. This was just another example of Carl's ability to recognize a great possibility, capitalize on it and watch it grow. Few bestsellers have such an incredible survival rate.

In stature, Carl was about five feet, ten inches, with a strong, wiry build; light hair blond to brown in color; and blue eyes. His grandson Carl III remembers him as a man who smiled a lot and had a sunny disposition and a generous spirit, not surprising in one who lived life on simple terms. He strongly believed that one never gets enough of something he doesn't need, and although in later years he could have afforded a higher-priced model, he said all he needed was a Chevrolet.

Carl also had an inquiring mind, and he liked to explore his own possibilities, deciding one day that he would like to play the violin. Difficult as it must have been, he taught himself how to play, and he became sufficiently proficient that he became an active member of a chamber group. And, of course, there was the piano, because in the words of one family member, "Everyone had a piano." Making music may have resembled making candy, since getting the timing right meant harmony in both. Carl's mother must have realized early in his life that his lack of a formal education would only act as a spur to fulfilling many ambitions.

FAMILY MAN

Although Carl wasn't particularly religious as a Christian Scientist, he was active as a Mason, which had a strong presence in North Denver. When he died, his obituary reported that he had been a member of Highland Masonic Lodge No. 86, Royal Arch Masons Rocky Mountain Consistory No. 2, El Jebel Shrine, Order of Eastern Star Temple Chapter No. 96 and the Knights Templar, and his family suggested contributions to the Shrine Crippled Children fund.[45] These associations meant that Carl and his family were always very connected with what went on in North Denver.

Carl was a family man in the best sense of the term, and he raised his children, as he had been raised, to understand the responsibilities one inherited as a son or daughter. Just as he had been allowed to make his own decision to abandon high school and strike out on his own, he allowed his son, Tom, the same latitude. Although he wasn't a hard taskmaster, he did believe that first came one's responsibilities.

Working at the store wasn't a choice for Tom or his sister, Marjorie, nor was it only an expectation on Carl Sr.'s part—it was a given. The factory was an integral part of the family's life and livelihood, and everyone was expected to contribute. When Carl and Laura were first married, home and workplace formed a unit, with the store in front, the candy kitchen to the rear and the living quarters upstairs, a common arrangement for family-owned and run businesses. Once they bought their first home, however, Laura had to bring Tom and Marjorie with her while she sold the candy. From an early age, when the children had grown past the toddler years, they were expected to pitch in and perform any small tasks that fit their chubby hands and legs. In the beginning, that might mean fetching the bags for a customer's purchases or, as each child became taller and stronger, sweeping the floors, wiping the counters or any other chore that made life easier for their parents. In the words of Carl's grandchildren, "It was simply what one did."

For young Tom, in about fifth or sixth grade that meant a walk to the rail yard, where he would sell candy bars to anyone willing to buy, whether it was laborers on their lunch break or transients who were just hanging around, hoping for a handout or lucky enough to have a spare five cents to hand over for a chocolate treat. At times it must have been a frightening experience, because men who are cold, hungry and homeless can be mean or dangerous. But many of the hobos, as they were called, were just sad people, "down and out" due to unfortunate circumstances brought about by bad economic times; the stories they told Tom must have taught him life lessons he would never otherwise have learned. They would certainly have given him an added appreciation of his own home life. By then, there were always candy bars available for him to sell, since the company had started to make them for the wholesale market.

One of Tom's favorite stories about his early sales experience occurred when he was dating a girl in high school and eventually met her parents. The girl's father kept eyeing Tom suspiciously and finally said, "You know, you remind me a lot of a little rugrat selling candy bars that used to run out of my warehouse." Tom simply smiled and said, "Gee, I don't remember anything like that," and quickly changed the subject to football at North High School. It didn't turn into a long-term relationship—surprise, surprise.

But just selling to the men who were coupling or uncoupling the rail cars or unloading freight would have given Tom a new perspective on different ways men earned their livelihoods. There is also a good chance he added to his vocabulary, but not words he could have brought home to his mother. Most important to Carl Sr., however, would have been the opportunity he was giving his son to strike out on his own, as he and his father, Peach, had done before him.

Chapter 5

Second Generation

A Hammond Jr.

By the time Tom graduated from North High School (where he excelled as an offensive lineman on the football team, participated in drama and an *a cappella* choir and was elected head boy), Carl was almost forty-five years old and could be proud that he had founded and run a successful business for almost twenty years. He and Laura had built a flourishing partnership in both marriage and the company, and it wouldn't have been surprising if Carl had looked forward to relinquishing some of his responsibilities to Tom. But Carl always respected an independent streak and must have recognized it in his own son—perhaps he also took a certain pride that Tom had graduated from North High School and wanted to attend college. As a result, Tom entered the Colorado School of Mines with the intention of studying geophysics, but unfortunately, he was only able to study one year there before World War II intervened.

Denver's location, far from any coasts, encouraged an isolationist attitude, and much of the population did not support President Roosevelt's view that the United States should support Great Britain's war effort. In fact, the *Denver Post* encouraged this kind of attitude in its readership in a statement: "If another war is coming, let's wait for it to arrive this time instead of going out to meet it."[46] However, by the time Pearl Harbor

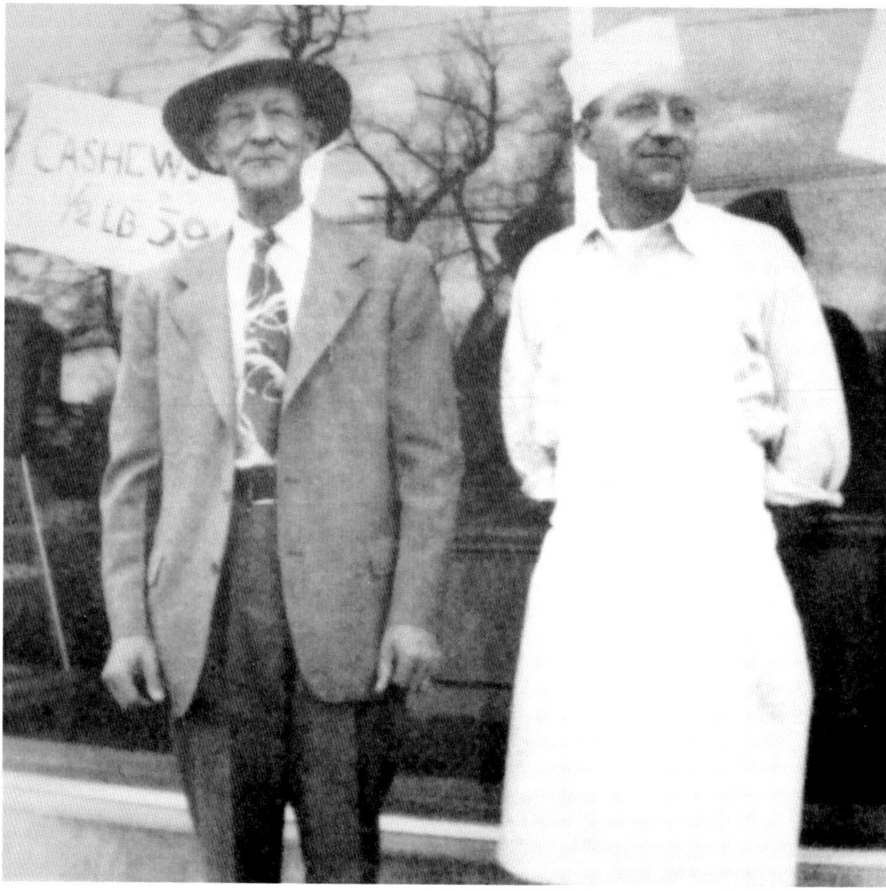

occurred, an editorial prophesied, "Japan started it. The United States will finish it."[47]

Candy makers like Carl must have been unnerved when the threat of sugar rationing loomed. It was actually the first commodity to be so treated, but in the end it was only individual consumers, and not manufacturers, who were affected. "Since the 1920s, the candy industry had promoted its product as a food ideally suited for every energy need. The war mobilization provided yet another opportunity to highlight the 'fatigue fighting' potential. In 1944, the NCA (National Confectioners' Association) ran eye-catching advertisements featuring a gleaming wrench surrounded by gumdrops and caramels under the banner 'Candy: food for work.'"[48] The juxtaposition is striking: by showing a steel tool next to confectionery, the consumer sees that candy is just as powerful and just as essential as the

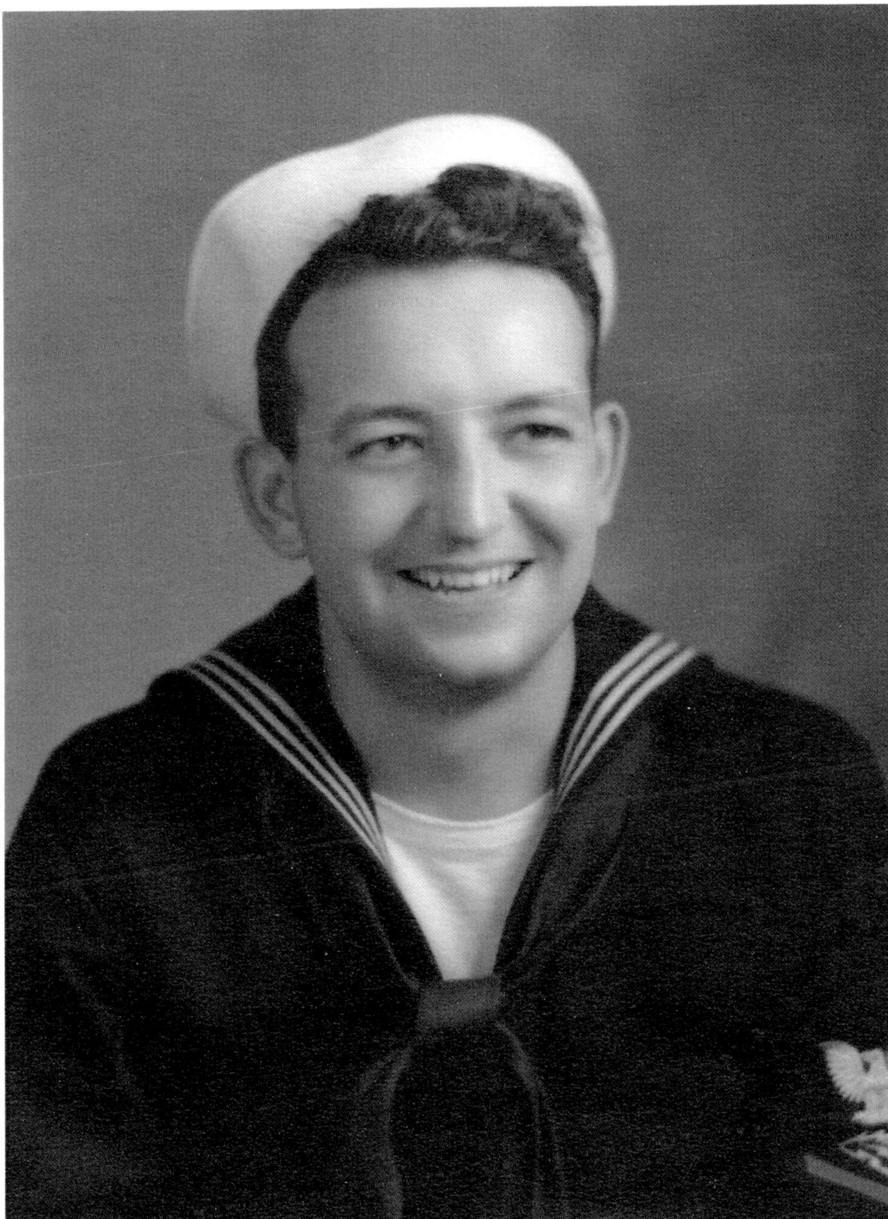

Above: A youthful Tom in his naval uniform during World War II. *Carl T. Hammond III Family Collection.*

Opposite: Carl Sr. and his son, Tom, in about 1923. *Hammond's Candies Collection.*

sturdy wrench. It was probably the kind of big business promotion that Carl would have abhorred, but he never saw any need to advertise, since he knew the quality of his products was his best sales tool. As it turned out, some canny grocery shoppers bought items like Hammond's peppermint pillows to sweeten their tea to avoid using up the small amounts in their sugar bowls. If that suited their taste buds, some may have brought them to any restaurants they frequented, since the owners were only allowed to serve one teaspoon per customer.[49]

As the end of his first year at Mines approached, Tom, like his father before him, and in the company of most of his able-bodied peers, had to abandon his plans and enter the service. Again, the Hammond spirit of self-reliance took over, and rather than wait for Uncle Sam and the draft board to determine his future, Tom enlisted in the navy, where he served as an electronics technician. He was going to have firsthand experience with the *Post*'s ultimatum. Starting with the lowly rank of seaman, Tom received several promotions to become a chief petty officer, serving on the USS *Franklin*, one of twenty-four Essex class aircraft carriers built during World War II. It had been commissioned in January 1944 and had served in several campaigns in the Pacific War, earning four battle stars.[50] The carrier was badly damaged by a Japanese air attack in March 1945, with the loss of over eight hundred of its crew, becoming the most heavily damaged United States carrier to survive the war. Fortunately, Tom came home uninjured, but by the time he was mustered out, he had to rethink his plans for further education. While on duty in California and enjoying himself at the USO, he had met June Jones, fallen in love and become engaged. As a result, Tom again joined his father at Hammond's Candies, and a new era began. The father-son mix of the two Carls, both strong-minded individuals, could have been fraught with impending disaster or, at best, existed with an uneasy truce. But, as the third Carl describes the family, "We are also easygoing." He never saw the two disagree because they didn't want to spend their time on negative energy.

THE SECOND FACTORY

Shortly after World War II ended, when shortages became less critical, Carl and his brother Harry once again partnered as builders, constructing a new factory in North Denver at Bryant Street and West Twenty-ninth

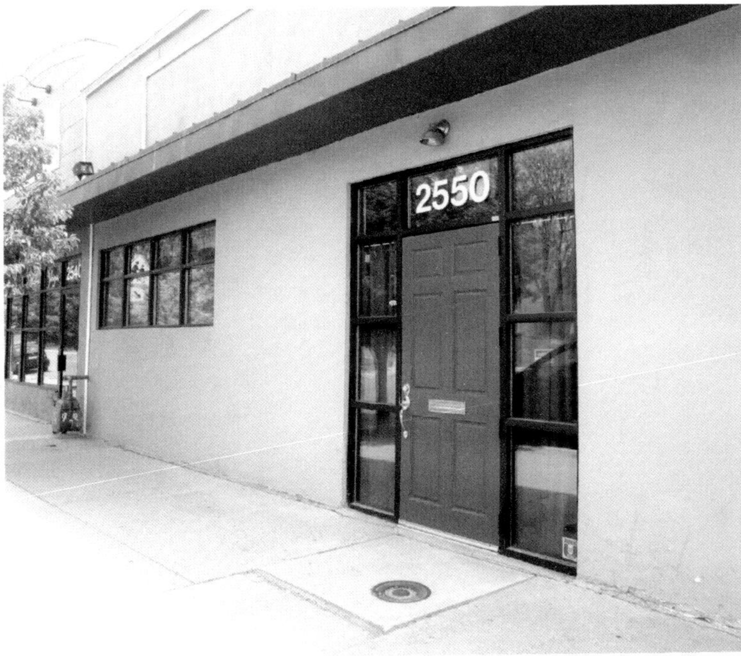

The site of the second factory, built by Carl Sr. and his brother Harry in about 1945 on Bryant Street, is now a condominium. *Photo by the author.*

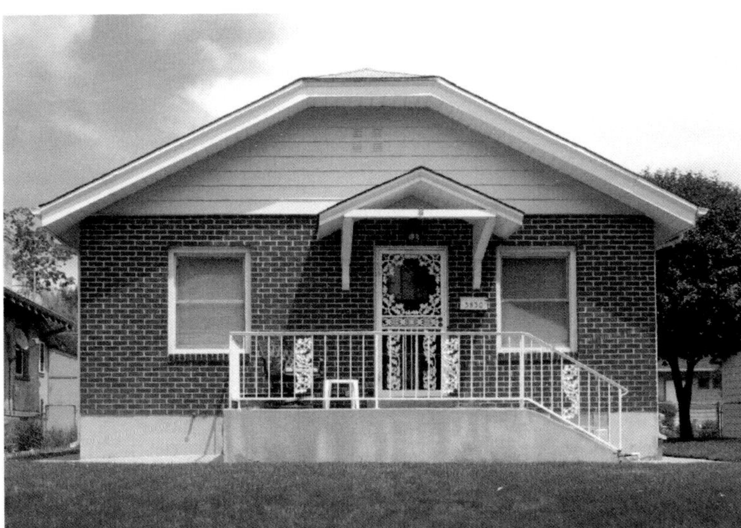

Carl and Laura Hammond's home on Newton Street. *Photo by the author.*

Avenue to replace the original one, which had finally become too small for the expanding operation. Even then, Carl Sr. required little in the way of fancy office equipment. He located his modest thirty- by thirty-six-inch desk underneath the stairs, where he continued to keep a handwritten ledger detailing the hours, pay and social security information of each employee. Carl and Laura had moved in about 1927 from Clay Street to a house on Newton Street, and at about the same time the brothers put up the new plant, they also built a second house at 3836 Newton Street. Tom and Marjorie grew up there, and it remained in the Hammond family until Laura's death.

Carl and Laura welcomed the newlyweds home when they returned from their wedding in California in October 1945 and were overjoyed to meet their first grandchild, Carl Thomas Hammond III, in December 1946. Carl, in turn, was joined by George in 1949, Keith in 1951, Patrick in 1953 and June and Tom's only daughter, Robin, born in 1960. June managed her large household by herself but could never have been considered a stay-at-home mom since, according to her children, she was involved in a multitude of organizations. Among her more time-consuming volunteer positions was as a tour guide for the Colorado Museum of Natural History (now the Denver Museum of Nature and Science), where she would frequently function as the guide for bus trips to the newly opened Air Force Academy in Colorado Springs. When she had accepted Tom's proposal, she had done so with one mild stipulation: that she be able to return to California annually to see her family. Her children enjoy their memories of the long train rides through the Rocky Mountains to Stockton, California, to be with their maternal grandparents in Escalon.

In 1950, when the Korean Conflict broke out, the U.S. Navy recalled Tom to active duty, and before his request for exemption from service could be acted upon, he had already reached Hawaii. There he received the good news that he could return home. When his ship sailed into the harbor, June, visibly pregnant, was there on the dock, their two young sons clinging to her hands. "Hi, Daddy," two-year-old George cried out as the first sailor approached. "Hi, Daddy," he repeated over and over again, becoming a bit bewildered as streams of sailors passed him by. Finally, as he grew a little tearful, the right daddy scooped him up in his arms, and his little world righted itself. It must have felt the same way to June, who had undoubtedly wondered how she was going to manage without Tom.

After living with Carl and Laura for about a year, Tom and June had moved to a duplex at 3124 West Twenty-fourth Street that June

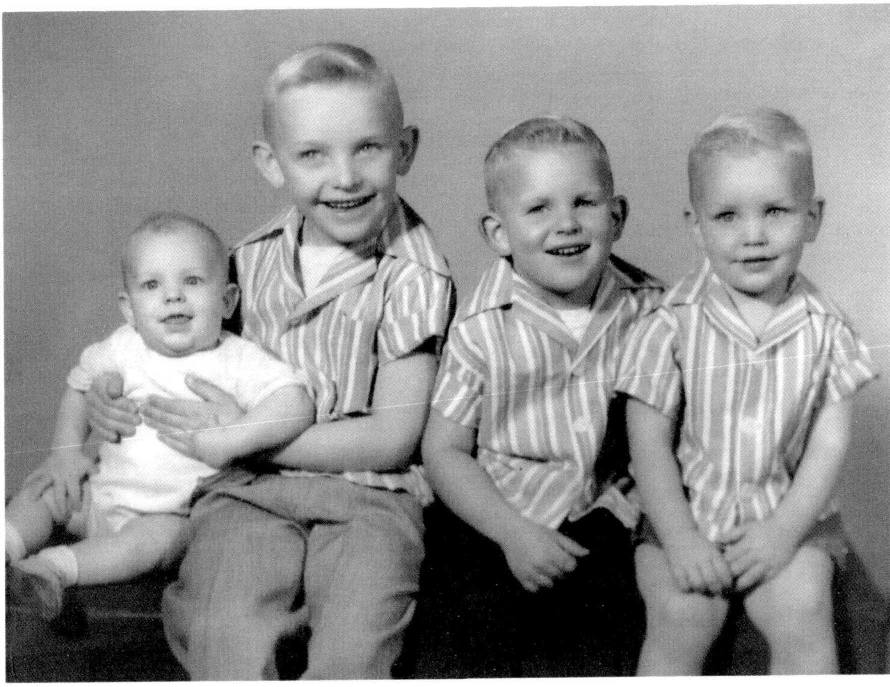

Carl Hammond III with younger siblings George, Keith and Patrick. *Carl T. Hammond III Family Collection.*

affectionately called the "dirty double." After four successful years at the candy factory, and with three boys under the age of five and a fourth on the way, they were ready for larger quarters.

Tom then bought the house at 2131 Grove Street, and his growing brood attended the Boulevard Elementary at Federal Boulevard and West Twenty-fourth Avenue, continuing on to Lake Junior High School, which is located, as its name would indicate, near Sloan Lake. Although the grammar school was eventually closed and refurbished as apartments, the middle school still graces the area with a campus one expects to find in movies and romantic teen novels. In style, Tom's house was a modest Denver bungalow, typical of the architecture of its time and area. June would have been very pleased with the location, since it was only a short distance to the Merritt United Methodist Church, where she and the children worshiped. Like many family homes, what had seemed spacious at first became somewhat crowded as the young Hammond boys grew, and by the time of Robin's birth, her crib shared space in Carl III's bedroom.

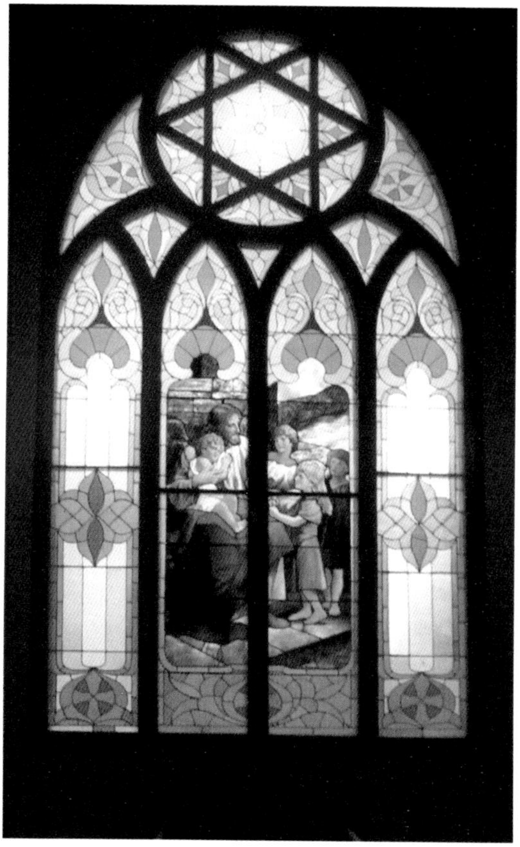

A stained-glass window at Merritt United Methodist Church, where June Hammond and her children worshiped. *Carl T. Hammond III Family Collection.*

History repeated itself. The next generation, in the Hammond tradition, was expected to pitch in at the factory and gradually learn the family business. It was a blessing in many ways, since it offered memories of their grandfather and great-grandfather they would otherwise have missed. Even before he was eight years old, Carl III remembers seeing Peach sweeping floors. By the time Carl was thirteen, he would be at the factory on weekends, washing the dishes and utensils, mopping the floor, weighing the batches. This continued through his junior high school years. It was part of the family credo—you were not paid; you worked because you were part of the family business; that's what you were supposed to do. However, there was also a curious twist to this arrangement. If you wanted to do something else, that was okay, too, but you had to bankroll whatever you wanted to do. Whatever your choice, you were guaranteed your necessities—room, board, clothes, school materials, etc. It worked pretty much this way both as a child of Carl and a child of Tom.

LIFE LESSON

Carl III recounts that he learned an important life lesson one day. A conversation that he overheard when he was in high school underscored for him just how much his grandfather valued being his own boss and knowing who he was and what he was about. As Carl III sat in the chair next to his grandfather's desk, all that he could hear were Carl Sr.'s very sparing responses to whoever was talking on the other end of the phone. The other gentleman's comments seemed quite detailed in comparison to Carl Sr.'s words:

> *"Oh, good morning, sir…Hmmm…Really?…How would that work?… Really?…That would take some thinking…Not sure that would be possible… It would take a lot of changes…Oh, now, I don't think so…Oh, I couldn't do that…Oh, if you think so…I understand…OK then…Goodbye."*
>
> *Carl Sr. sat there quietly, shaking his head, a little lost in thought. Finally, he looked up at his grandson with a somewhat puzzled look on his face as if to say, "How could anyone, who ever conducted business with me, think I would even consider the proposition I just refused?"*
>
> *"That was Denver Dry Goods," he explained, not having to clarify to Carl III the value of having a contract with the preeminent department store in the city. "We've been selling them our peanut brittle. Guess they think we're pretty good, because now they want us to supply all their candy."*
>
> *Carl III gasped with excitement. "What did you tell him?"*
>
> *"I said I didn't want to do it."*
>
> *"What did they say?" his confused grandson asked.*
>
> *"Then they can't buy candy from us anymore. That's OK."*
>
> *Carl III just exclaimed, "What?" That is when his grandfather succinctly professed his whole business philosophy.*
>
> *"I can't make all the candy for Denver Dry Goods. I'd have to build a factory. I've never borrowed a dime in my life. I don't know how to run a factory like that, and besides that, what would happen if they decided to give the business a year later to Russell Stover or another company? Then I would be working for them. That's all."*

Another candy company did get that contract, and just as Carl had feared could happen to him if he overextended, that company went out of business. To add to the irony of that situation, Hammond's bought two copper kettles at that company's liquidation sale.

Carl knew what he wanted and what he was about. He explained to his young relative that if more than 25 or 30 percent of his business was for another company, in reality he would be working for them. He would never do that, for it would mean breaking his own personal code of professional conduct. He would always and only be his own man.

CANDY WAGES

Carl III likes to tell a story on himself that reveals that he really did get paid, as he often ate half a pound of candy in wages. His favorite was the cashew brittle, which he would watch his father make as he poured the twenty-five pounds of cashew-laden candy syrup onto the steel slab. There it would sit like a large mound of cookie dough slowly cooling. If left unattended, the cashew-syrup mix would harden, requiring a jackhammer to break it into bite-size pieces. Instead, Tom would use a metal tube about two feet long and six inches in diameter and roll it across the batch, much like rolling out a pie crust, flattening the cashew-syrup mix into a layer of brittle no thicker than a single cashew. He would then press it down and pull it apart. At this point, it would still be warm but cool enough to break off a piece to taste. This was the moment Carl III found it to be the most delicious. Minutes later, it would be completely cool, losing the magnificence of warm candy.

Tasting the candy was a requirement. Jo Anne, Carl III's future wife, worked at the candy factory during her high school days. She fondly remembers Carl Sr. taking her aside on her first day with this admonition: "Our candy needs to be of the highest quality or people won't buy it. So you're expected to taste the candy as it's being made, so we'll know that it meets our expectations." And then with a smile he added, "Don't feel guilty tasting whatever candy you want."

Carl III carried the candy tasting a little too far. In his younger years, and with a certain amount of guilt, he would try to sneak into the chocolate room, where he would stuff a chocolate raisin cluster, a cherry cordial and a Piggy Back (commonly known as a Turtle™) into his mouth all at once. He described the cluster as a supersized kiss. For all that, he never gained a pound, but he did become his dentist's best friend. Although Carl III was good at listening to his father's wisdom, it is doubtful he would have heeded the advice that Tom gave in an interview with the *Denver Post* many years later: "What candy is, is a concentrated food. If people will eat candy when they are working, it tastes good and does you a lot of good. It has dextrose sugar and protein and it does you a lot of good…But if you eat it while sitting down and playing bridge or watching TV, that sugar that you would normally use up is deposited as fat. Work with sensible dental hygiene and don't overdo it and make a glutton of yourself."[51]

What Could Be Sweeter?

The chocolate room was a special part of the factory where Tom's children could admire true artistry. The centerpiece was a table about three by five feet, and the chocolate dippers sat on each side with a marble slab in front of them. In the center of the table was a recessed pan, rather like a small well, that held melted chocolate that was kept warm by a light bulb. The chocolate dippers would pull chocolate out of the pan and spread it on the marble slab, continually working the chocolate with their right hands until the chocolate cooled to the proper temperature and consistency to allow the chocolate to "seed" (cool without the cocoa butter separating and causing bloom, or white spots, on the chocolate). The chocolate dippers would then use their left hands to pick up the cherry cordial (cherry covered with fondant), or whatever they were working on that day, and drop it into the chocolate on the slab; use their right hands to cover the cherry cordial with chocolate; lift the cherry cordial out of the chocolate; and drop the now chocolate-covered confection onto a tray to cool. It is the interaction of the cherry with the fondant that produces the liquid in the candy. When the cherry cordial is dropped on the tray, a string of chocolate naturally follows the chocolate dipper's finger as she lifts her hand and is used to create a design on the top of the candy. Each string needs to be different to identify it from all the other candies such as vanilla or chocolate cream. On a day the dippers were producing creams, Tom would make an approximately thirty-pound batch about the consistency of cookie dough. The batch would be put into the hopper of a depositor machine, which would drop little button-like blobs of the mixture onto the tray. The trio of Alice, who formed the centers and set it up for the chocolate dipper, Mary Kohler, who dipped, and Mary Ford, who packed the candies, often crops up in Hammond's Candies stories.

It is a common fact in the annals of handmade candy that a person with a warm skin temperature can never be a dipper, since that would influence the consistency of the chocolate.

To create marshmallow for the Mitchell Sweets, the candy makers poured the egg whites and syrup into a kettle about three and a half feet in diameter and about two feet high. Using a mixer about five feet tall, they would whip the mixture at an incredible speed until it formed high peaks. With giant spatulas, they would then spread it on a table covered with waxed brown paper—it had a consistency that was lighter than frosting but heavier than meringue. When it cooled, it was ready to be turned over and cut into long ten-inch strips. The tool to cut the marshmallow was unique. It

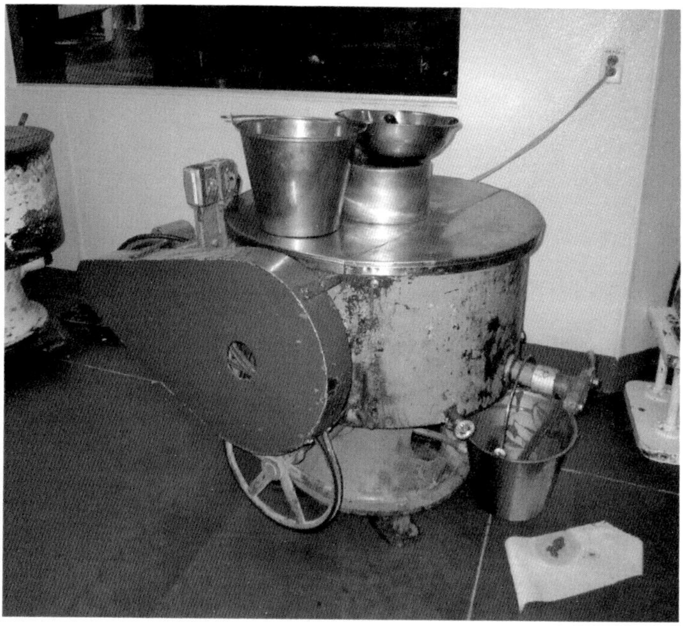

The old chocolate melter is still in continuous use. *Photo by the author.*

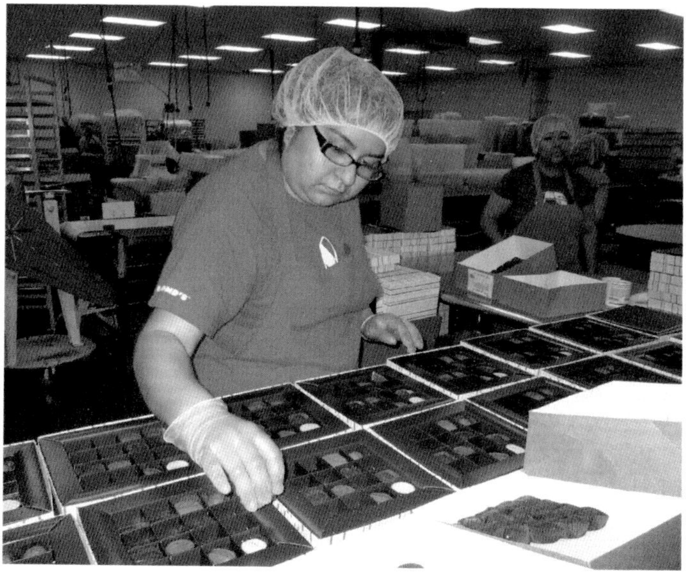

Each chocolate is placed in a paper cup and then decoratively boxed. *Photo by the author.*

consisted of circular steel discs spaced two inches apart on a heavy steel rod about two feet long and was "rolled" across the marshmallow. After drying overnight, the ten-inch marshmallow strips were then dipped in warm caramel and placed on a cooling slab. Scissors were used to cut the caramel-dipped marshmallow strips into one-inch-wide pillows, and they were hand-wrapped in wax paper to complete the finished Mitchell Sweet. The process takes three days to complete.

Tom always modeled not only candy-making methods like this but also his business practices on what he had learned from Carl, which might explain how the two talented men were able to get along so well. From the time he started the company, Carl never took a salary, putting his profits back into the company and presumably bringing home what Laura would need for food and the general upkeep of the children and house. From the time he had any discretionary income, Carl also invested steadily and profitably in oil stocks so that in the future, he and Laura could live off the dividends. He then took money only when he needed it for taxes. At some point, Carl and Tom set up a partnership, but Tom imitated his father and never took any salary either, giving June a monthly stipend. She was known to complain that there was usually too much month at the end of her money.

Carl had the reputation of being a very patient man, always available to help his grandchildren perfect their technique as they were gradually allowed to graduate from sweeping the floors to assisting in the candy production. Carl and Tom continued to be in charge of creating the suckers, for example, but the next generation might insert the sticks into the lollipops or crook the canes. When the boys grew taller and more muscular, they would help pour the batch for brittle or the hard candies being made that day.

A Loyal Boss

Even today, it is remembered that the folks who worked for Tom seemed to genuinely care about him, and despite the fact that he didn't pay very much, they all stayed many years at Hammond's. In 1983, Tom had three employees who were over eighty, and more importantly, they were productive and happy to be working. Tom's relationships with his employees and his children followed parallel paths, since both genuinely liked to be with him. Despite all his business dealings, Tom never had an enemy, and people knew he would not be insulted; he maintained you could be insulted only if you wished to be.

He had a firm belief in the power of attitude. In many ways, Tom mirrored the thoughts of Robert Burns when he wrote in "A Man's a Man for A' That": "Then let us pray that come it may (As come it will for a' that,) That Sense and Worth, oer a' the earth…Shall brothers be for a' that."[52]

One particular anecdote underscores how Tom inspired loyalty in the people who came to work at Hammond's and shows in an interesting manner that he could understand their desire to attempt new endeavors in a way that echoed the Hammond family spirit of self-sufficiency.

Tommy Williams was a candy maker who had worked for Hammond's Candies for well over fifteen years when he was approached by a wholesale customer to work directly for them making Piggy Backs (similar to Turtles™). The wholesaler had developed a booming business selling snacks and candy door to door in large industrial office complexes throughout Denver. Piggy Backs were one of its best-selling products, and the company knew it could make them for less than it cost to buy them from Hammond's. So the company lured Tommy Williams away with a lucrative deal. Unfortunately, in the wholesaler's zeal to cut out the middle man, it neglected to do its homework, not realizing how precarious setting up a new business could be without a well thought out plan. The company invested heavily in equipment and signed a contract with a supplier of chocolate and nuts, taking advantage of the lower prices through bulk purchases. But it over ordered, and when sales of the Piggy Backs fell far below expectations, the company was left with a large quantity of now useless ingredients. Unable to break the contract, and with no cash to buy it out, the company was forced to close, which in other circumstances would have left Mr. Williams high and dry. But Tom Hammond was made of sterner stuff, and he welcomed Tommy and his expertise back to the company. Tommy never let another thought about leaving Hammond's enter his mind again. Once more, Tom was following the example Carl had set for him in allowing his workers to blaze their own trails. Years before, one of Carl's dippers, Bernice Williams (Tom Williams's wife), had left to start her own enterprise; Carl sold her the cream fondant she needed to make hand-dipped chocolates.

WORK ETHIC

Another story illustrates the work ethic that Tom practiced. As his years in the industry accumulated, he came to know many other manufacturers.

At some point, he became acquainted with a man named Goelitz who just happened to be a descendant of Gustav Goelitz, who in 1869 had founded the company that eventually came to be known for its Jelly Bellies. Mr. Goelitz called Tom one day, saying he was selling the Jelly Belly® distributorship for Denver, and asked whether Tom wanted to buy it.

"What's it going to take?" Tom asked.

"Oh, just an inventory of about thirty different flavors, maybe about 150 cases, then hiring a sales rep and a delivery man…," came the beginning of a response.

Before Mr. Goelitz could finish, and remembering his father's admonitions about how easily he could end up working for the other man, Tom declined the offer. Tom knew how to make candy. He didn't know how to warehouse, inventory, sell and distribute candy to hundreds of retailers. Ultimately, another individual bought the distributorship, making it a resounding success, and the Hammond family cheerfully, but without regrets, dubbed that chapter in their history "a fortune missed."

Several years later, with Jelly Bellies® flying off the shelves, an independent sales rep, also someone Tom knew, asked him for assistance in introducing the Jelly Belly® to a major Denver grocer. This would be a coup for the sales rep since there were a large number of stores in the Denver area. The only fly in the ointment was that the grocer demanded a direct purchasing relationship with Goelitz, thereby avoiding Goelitz's Denver distributor, which would lower the cost to the store. The store's executives argued that Goelitz would make even more money without a middleman because of the sales volume the grocery chain would provide. Mr. Goelitz declined, stating that they had an exclusive distributor agreement and future profitability was not a justification to break a prior commitment. Neither Goelitz nor Tom would consider any business deal that undermined their sense of fairness and honesty, and the sales rep was dumbfounded.

One has only to go to the Jelly Belly® Candy Company website to understand how similar in objectives and principles those two industry leaders were both in the manner in which they conducted their affairs and in how they protected the reputation of their companies. Of primary importance to both was the quality of the confections they produced, and they expected anyone with whom they did business to practice the same standards of honesty and integrity.

Just as Carl's family and employees praised him for his fair play, they recognized that he was a just man. He had acquired his factory and every piece of equipment in it through hard work and attention to detail, and he expected all of them to appreciate that fact. There were probably times when they wished he was less adept at keeping a mental inventory of everything. If a worker was boiling syrup and wanted to check the temperature, he would usually use a thermometer to check if it had reached the proper heat. However, if he had the misfortune to drop and break it, he was also expected to admit to the loss—and the cost of the thermometer was deducted from his paycheck. It didn't matter that there might be several more in a supply closet because everyone owned the responsibility for the company's profitability. In that sense, Hammond's was somewhat similar to a cooperative.

Debt Is Death

Having survived the Great Depression, and believing unequivocally that debt was death, neither Carl nor Tom ever borrowed any money to operate the business other than trade credit (ten to thirty days to pay for ingredients). They made great candy and sold it at a profit. Without debt to pay off, this profit directly translated into cash. Therefore, the cash balance in the bank could be used to manage their cash flow. They would only buy something when there was money in the bank. It sounds simple, but with the ups and downs of business, it gets complicated.

Their secret was understanding the cash flow cycle. At Hammond's, the money in the bank would be highest at the beginning of the summer. Summer was generally break-even time. As a result, this money would be used to produce inventory during the fall for the Christmas sales, and the cash would begin draining out. As the Christmas sales were collected, the cash would remain low while inventory was produced for Valentine's Day and Easter. This was a scary time. However, when the Easter sales were collected, the cash balance would build, and only then could they determine whether they were profitable.

The temptation, of course, was to spend some of the big bank balance during the summer to enhance their quality of life. However, being frugal by persuasion, any money determined to be surplus to requirements was not spent but, rather, invested in the stock market or manufacturing equipment. More importantly, the extra cash was used to carry the company through the inevitable lean years that destroyed a multitude of other small businesses.

Carl paid all the salaries in cash as well, with very few exceptions, but in that regard, he kept meticulous records. His ledger was a light gray cloth-

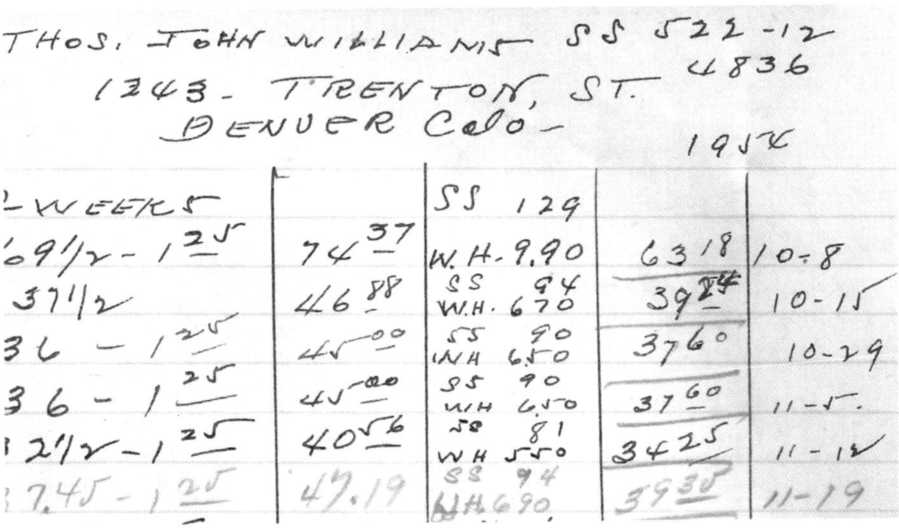

THOS. JOHN WILLIAMS SS 522-12 4836
1243 - TRENTON, ST.
DENVER COLO -
1956

2 WEEKS		SS 129		
69 1/2 - 1.25	74.37	W.H.-9.90	63.18	10-8
37 1/2	46.88	SS 94 W.H. 670	39.24	10-15
36 - 1.25	45.00	SS 90 WH 650	37.60	10-29
36 - 1.25	45.00	SS 90 WH 650	37.60	11-5
32 1/2 - 1.25	40.56	SS 81 WH 550	34.25	11-12
37.45 - 1.25	47.19	SS 94 WH 690	39.30	11-19

Carl Sr.'s ledger with Tommy Williams's salary data. *Carl T. Hammond III Family Collection.*

bound notebook about five by six and a half inches. In it, carefully written, usually in pencil but sometimes in pen, the pertinent information for each employee was listed. The worker's name, address and social security number were noted at the top of the page and then, in hand-ruled columns, the following information: in the first column, Carl listed the number of hours worked and the hourly rate; next, the total salary for the week; then the amount deducted for the social security payment; after that, the withholding figure; next to last was the net salary; in the final column was the month and day of the pay period. At first glance, the ledger for the years 1950–56 might seem a little confusing since many pages have entries that read 40/80 or 32/70. Translated simply, those numbers mean that the individual worked forty or thirty-two hours and was paid eighty or seventy cents an hour. Since the average hourly wage for all manufacturing jobs in 1950 was $1.59, Hammond's pay scale, while not princely, was well in line with most of the nation, However, to put the wage scale in perspective for twenty-first-century consumers, the average price for a half gallon of milk was forty-one cents, and a housewife (as she was then called) could buy five pounds of flour at the grocery store for forty-nine cents.[53]

The working conditions in the factory were, by the very nature of the product being made, uncomfortable. When the heat from a stove is strong enough to bring a kettle of syrup weighing almost seventy pounds to over

325 degrees, the room temperature soon reflects that, hovering anywhere from 90 to 100 degrees. Add to that the simple dynamic of strong, energetic individuals who are actively stirring and molding great slabs of candy blocks or scouring utensils and other equipment to get them ready for the next batch, and the room gets even warmer. It is important to realize as well that in an operation such as Hammond's, no one is working by himself. Every step is conducted in concert with the next one, and candy doesn't wait. Each procedure depends on the previous one, and timing is crucial. If syrup cools too much, it hardens and is useless to the candy maker who is waiting to add color or flavor, so the kitchen helpers need to be constantly alert to their part in the process. But in an almost magical way, both Carl and Tom instilled in their staff a sense of pride in the quality of their work, so that the daily discomforts diminished in everyone's eyes. Besides that, it is difficult to complain when the boss is working beside you and enduring the same conditions. Carl and Tom never missed a beat.

Chapter 6

Ending an Era

A Good Life Led

During the late 1940s and '50s when Tom was assisting Carl in running Hammond's Candies, it might have seemed like there was little variation in the operations, but one imperceptible change was taking place: Carl was undeniably getting older. Born in 1895, he had seen vast changes, from the Model T, to the Wright brothers at Kitty Hawk, to his own experiences during the horror of serving in World War I; he had lived through the Crash of 1929 and survived the Great Depression; he had sent his only son off to World War II; he had witnessed the dawn of antibiotics and the television age. When at the age of forty-two his sister, Mabel, had given birth to Paul, a son with Down's Syndrome, Carl, Harry and Tom had set up a trust so that Paul would always be assured of care.

Throughout this time, Carl had grown to adulthood, happily married and seen both his children and his company grow and flourish. If he felt tired, hardly anybody noticed, and he continued to appear at 2550 West Twenty-ninth Avenue every day.

On August 20, 1966, Carl and Laura's forty-sixth wedding anniversary, he suffered a fatal stroke. Carl indicated he would not be a vegetable, and he died the following Wednesday on August 24. In addition to his children, his brother, Harry, his sister, Mabel, and eight grandchildren survived him.

It was so sudden and unexpected that one grandson remembers he was building a ping-pong table when he heard the terrible news. Carl III describes his legacy this way:

> *I remember the bus ride home from the University of Denver as if it were yesterday, not fifty years ago. The nice thing about riding buses is it gives you a chance to think, and I was thinking about the death of my grandfather.*
>
> *What did it all mean?*
>
> *Unerringly I came back to one conversation. Two years earlier I had told him about my plans to attend the University of Denver to study accounting.*
>
> *He said fondly, "That's great. If you need anything like tuition or books, don't hesitate to ask. I'll help."*
>
> *I was stunned he would say such a thing, given how much he valued the idea that a person should work and pay for what he wants. So I replied, "No, that's ok. I can live at home, ride the bus to school, and work in the afternoons and summers to cover the tuition and books."*
>
> *In 1964, tuition at the University of Denver was $3,600 a year, books were roughly another $150. DU's School of Business was located in downtown Denver, so with only morning and evening classes, a student could find afternoon work in the plethora of professional offices within walking distance. It was eminently doable.*
>
> *Thirty years later it occurred to me that Grandfather had already given me everything I needed even before I entered DU. His life taught me the value of hard, honest work, and a desire to do things right. With those lessons I built a successful career in Public Accounting, followed by a progression of various financial management positions in the San Diego real estate industry.*
>
> *I am forever grateful.*

An era had ended. Tom continued much the same style of Carl's hands-on approach to running the factory, and in many ways, he continued to do it all as his father had. As he took over the reins completely, he continued the amazing feat of producing about 150 different kinds of candy in just about 1,400 square feet. The annual sales in 1968 were $110,000, with retail accounting for 21 percent and wholesale 79 percent. This would translate into $20,000 in sales for 1950 assuming a 10 percent growth rate (including inflation); with a 7 percent growth rate, 1950 sales would have been $32,000.

A product list for that time shows the enormity of the output.

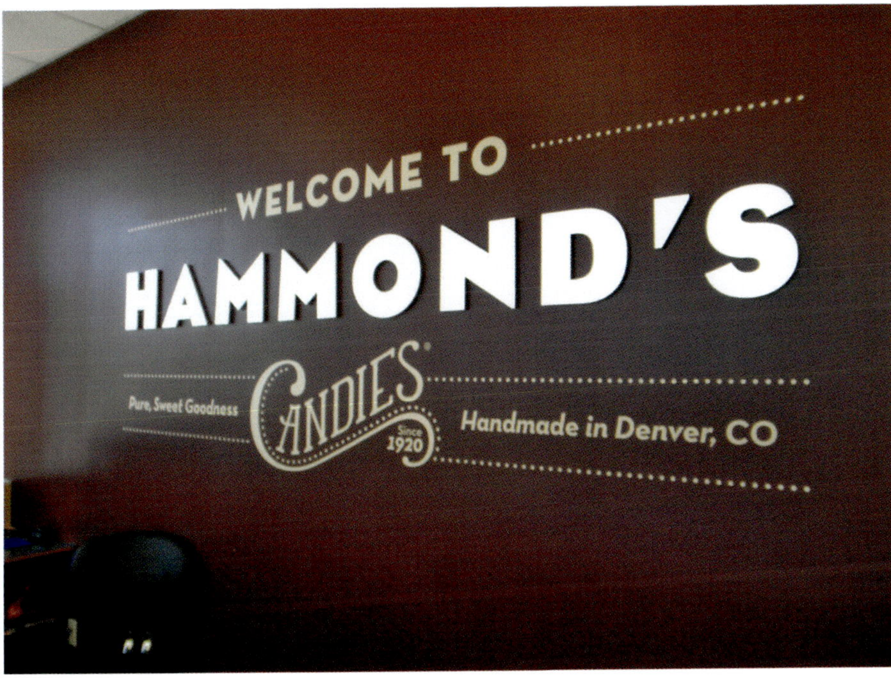

The Hammond's sign welcomes guests to the tour office. *Photo by Michael Scalisi.*

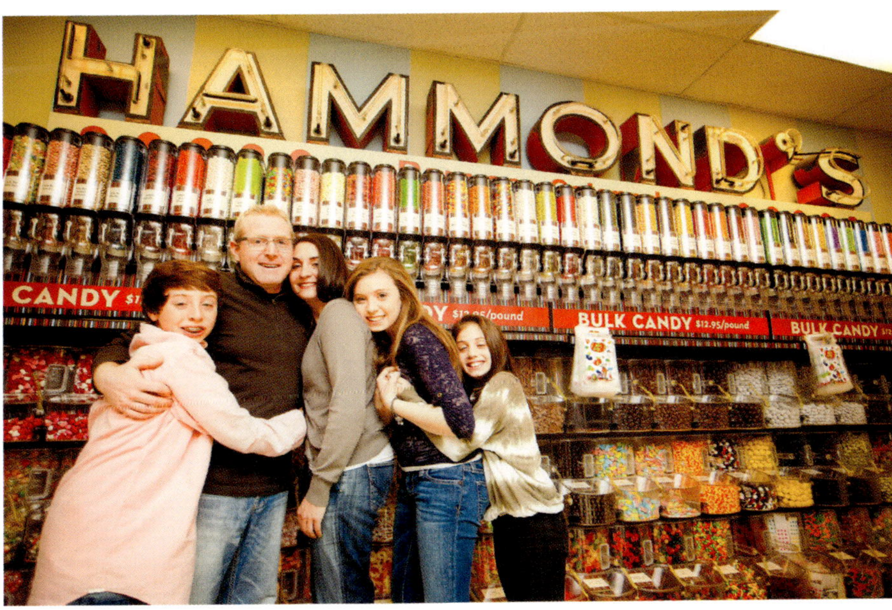

Hammond's CEO Andy Schuman with his wife, Lori, and their three children, Joey, Eliza and Abby. *Photo by McBoat Photography, Centennial, Colorado.*

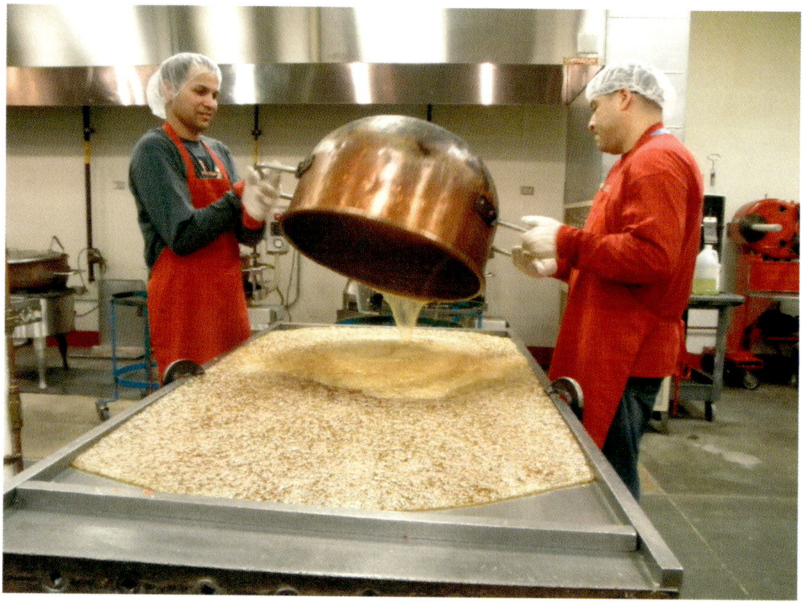

Pouring a batch of candy onto the cooling table for coloring and flavoring. *Photo by Michael Scalisi.*

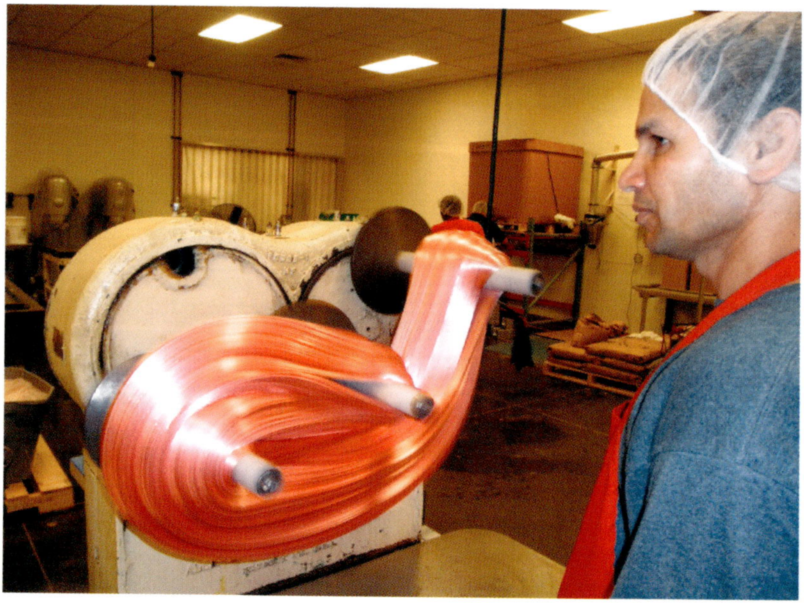

A candy puller, probably bought by founder Carl Hammond, used to trap air and lighten the color of the candy. *Photo by Michael Scalisi.*

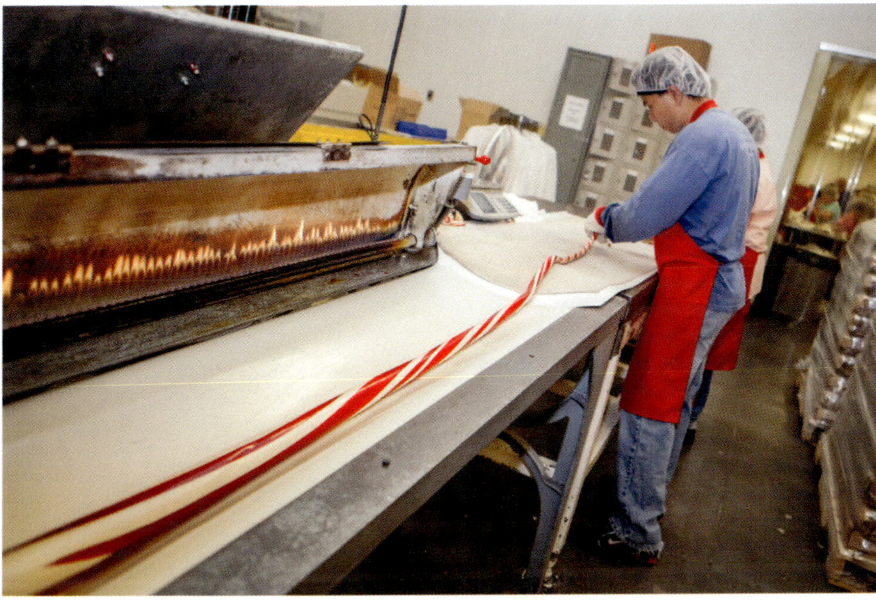

A cook at the batch roller hand shaping peppermint candy for canes. *Photo by McBoat Photography, Centennial, Colorado.*

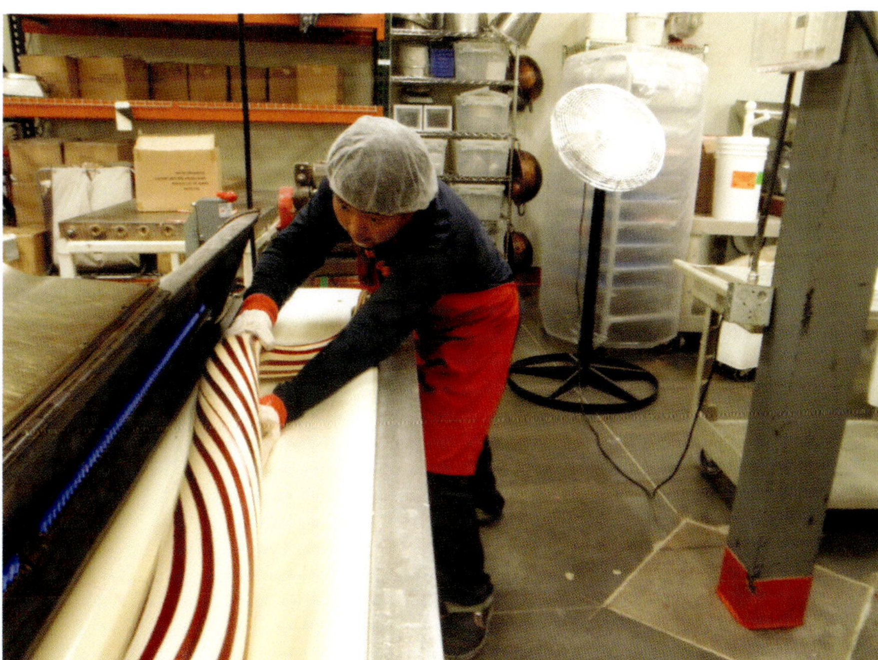

Candy on the gas-heated batch roller being hand shaped for the thin rope that will become peppermint cocoa stirrers. *Photo by Michael Scalisi.*

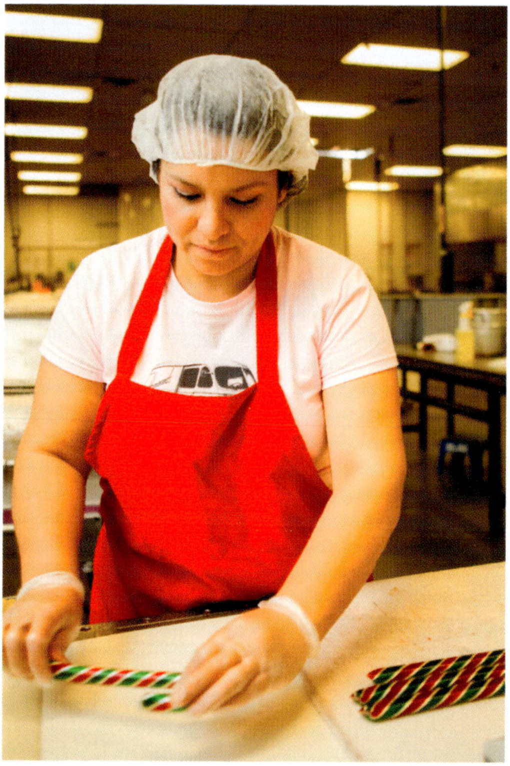

Left: A kitchen assistant forming a candy cane, Hammond's number-one all-time best-selling hard candy. *Photo by McBoat Photography, Centennial, Colorado.*

Below: Kitchen workers quickly inserting lollipop sticks while the candy remains pliable. *Photo by Michael Scalisi.*

Opposite, top: Ever-popular peppermint lollipops on their way to wrapping and sealing. *Photo by Michael Scalisi.*

Opposite, bottom: Candy stripes being molded to be run through the ribbon candy machine. *Photo by Michael Scalisi.*

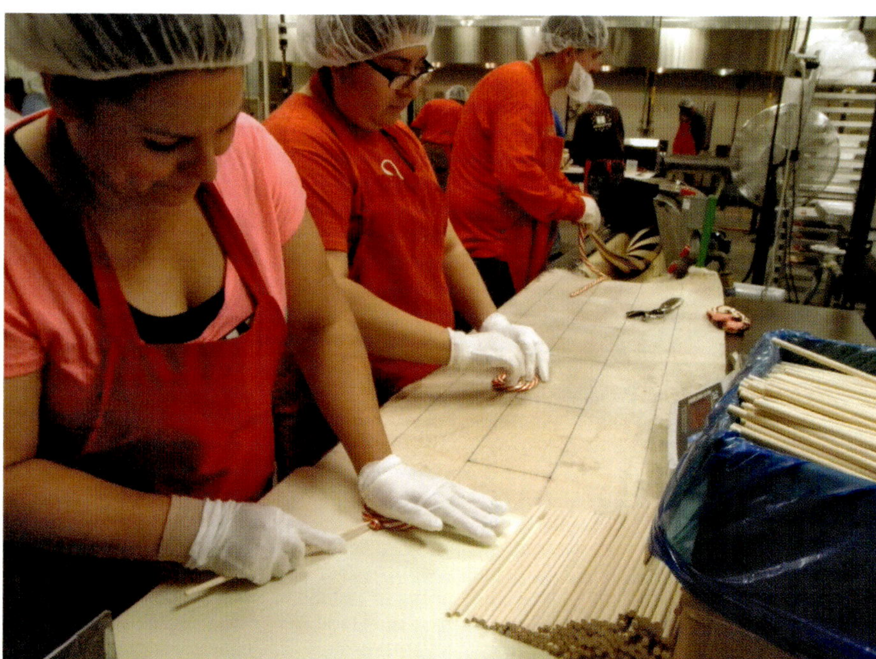

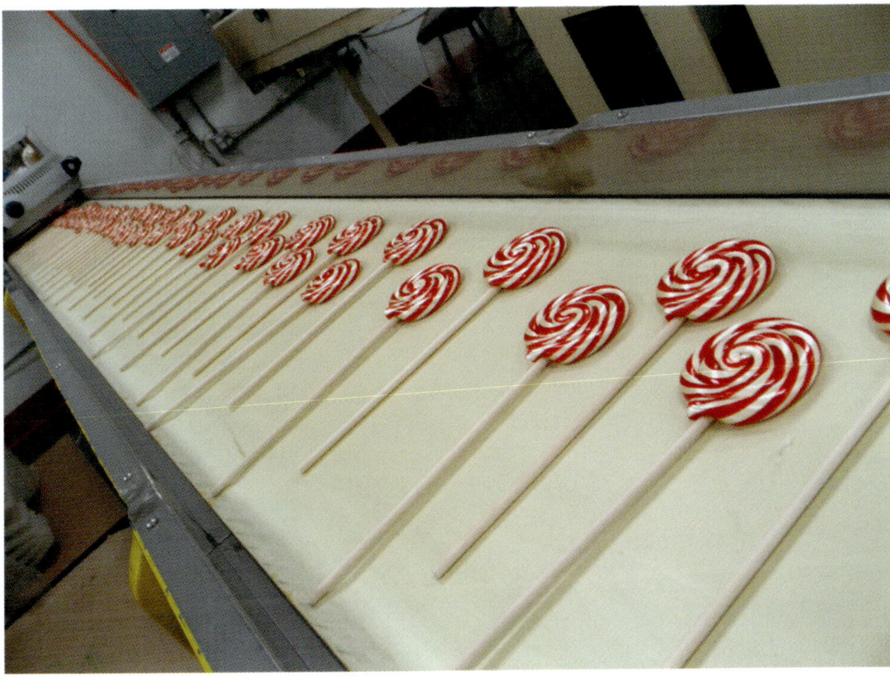

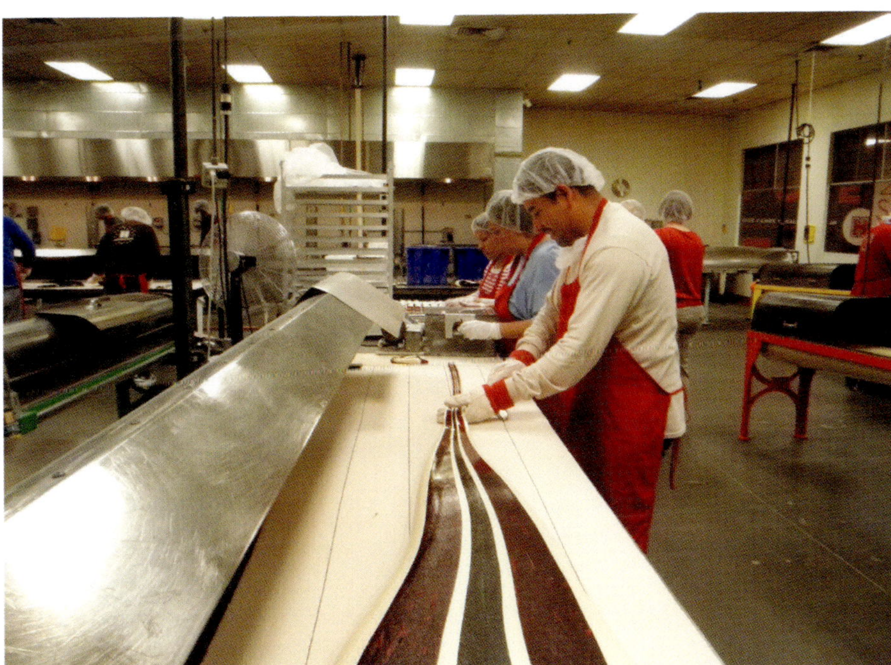

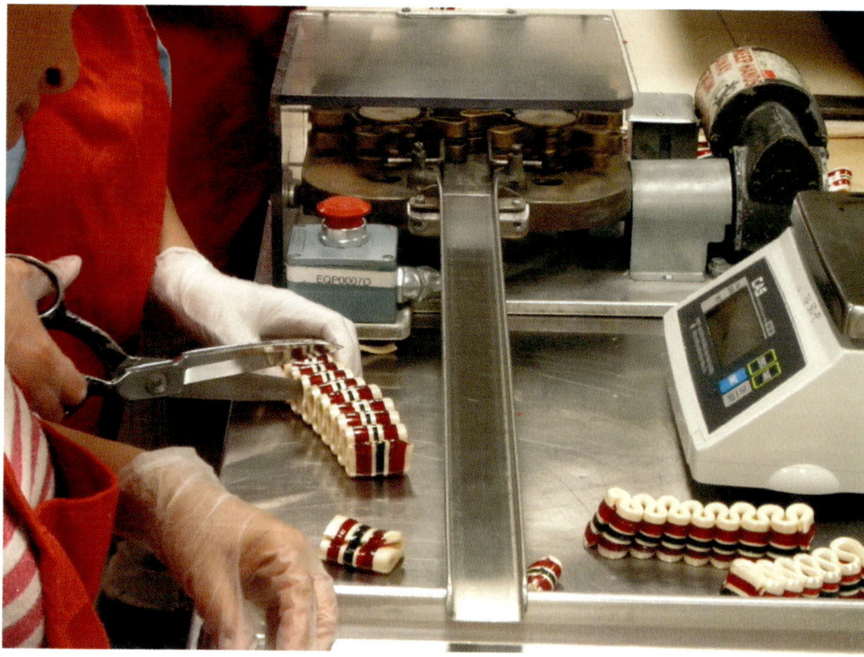

Large shears make the perfect cutting tool for the ribbon candy as it emerges from the crimping equipment. *Photo by Michael Scalisi.*

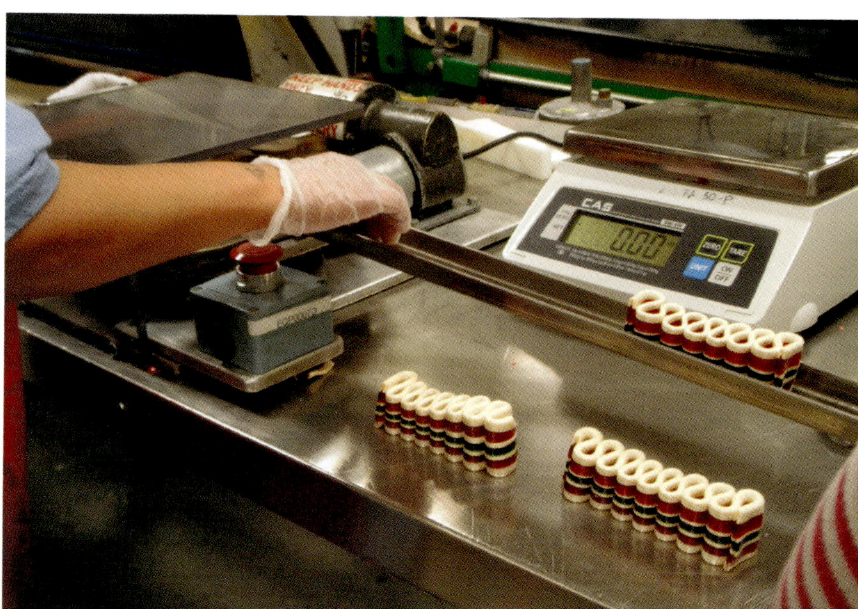

Cutting ribbon candy to the correct size for boxing. *Photo by Michael Scalisi.*

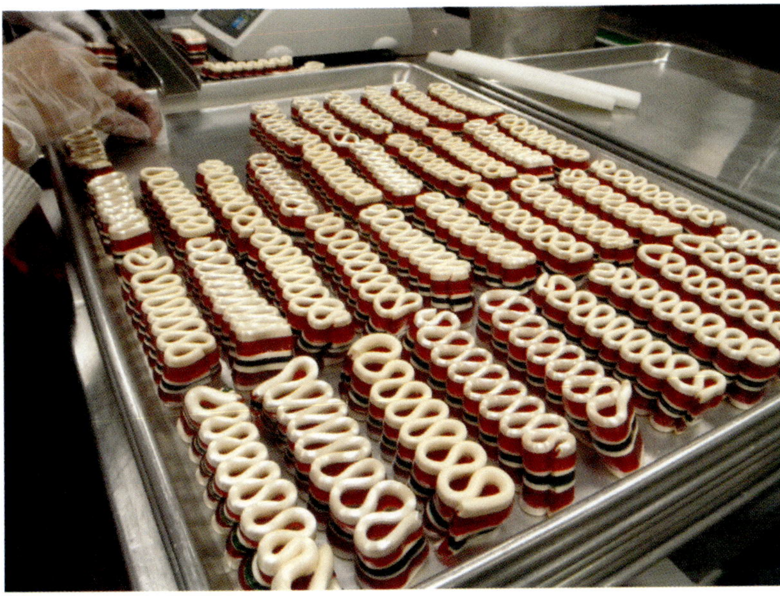

Trays of ribbon candies that have symbolized the holidays for countless generations. *Photo by Michael Scalisi.*

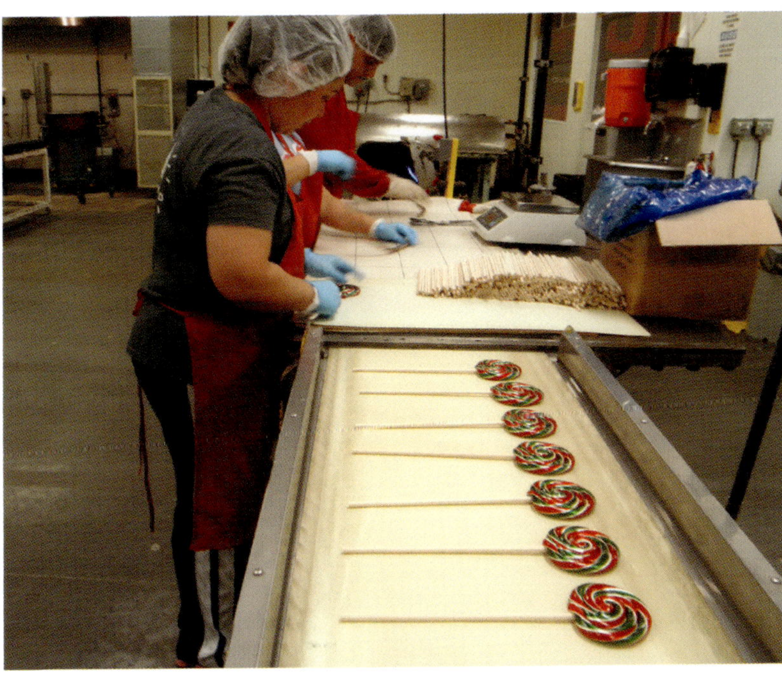

Multicolored lollipops ready for packaging. *Photo by Michael Scalisi.*

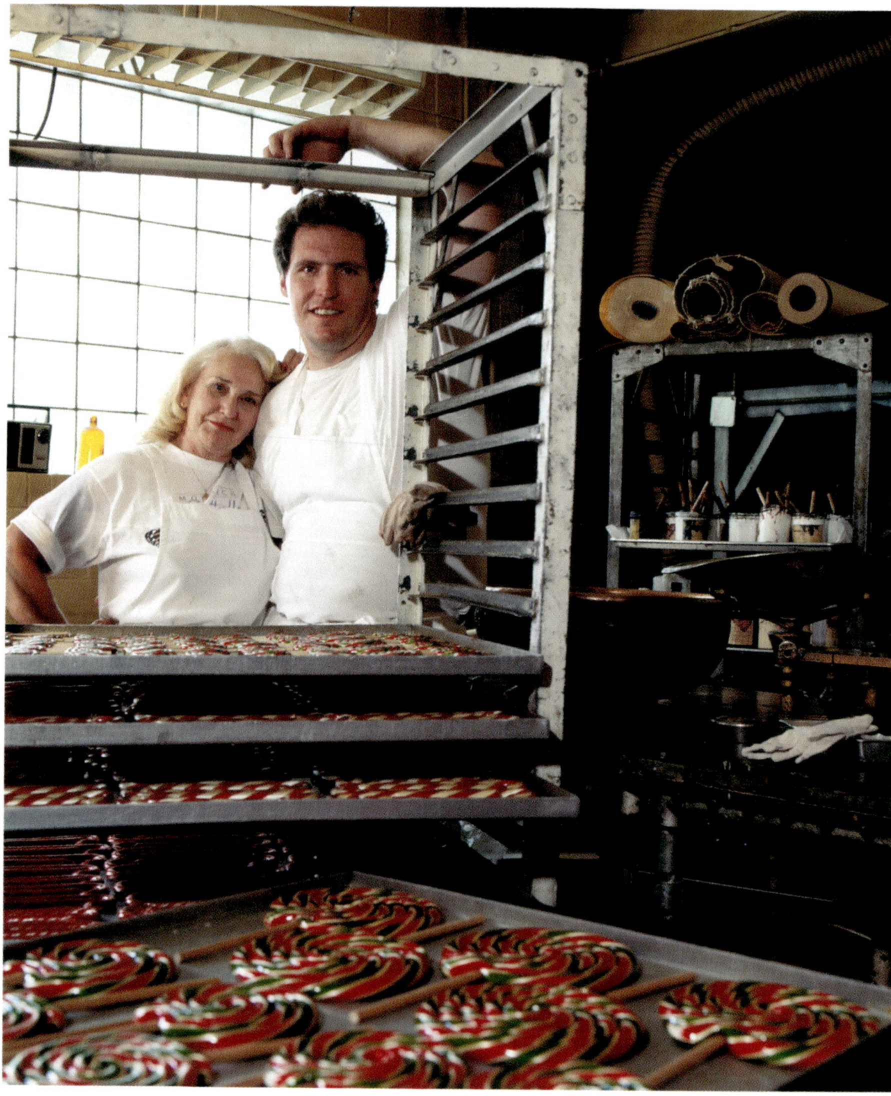

Owner June Hammond and son-in-law Emery Dorsey admiring trays of lollipops and candy canes in preparation for Christmas 1994. *Photography Dominique Vorillon.*

Opposite, top: Feeding a "rope" of hard candy into the cutting machine. *Photo by Michael Scalisi.*

Opposite, bottom: A tray of art candy, traditionally known as cut rock, awaits packaging. *Photo by Michael Scalisi.*

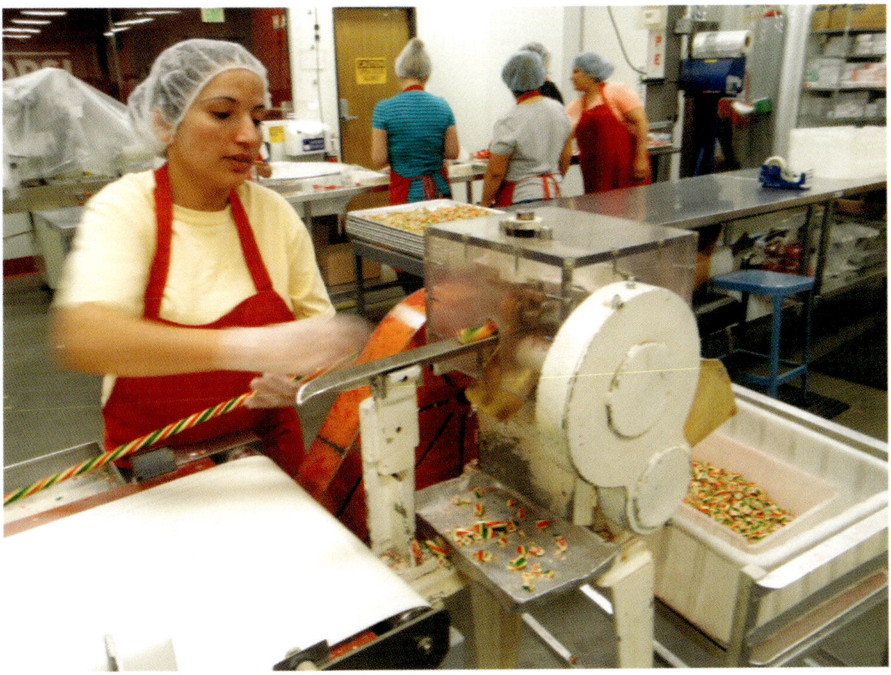

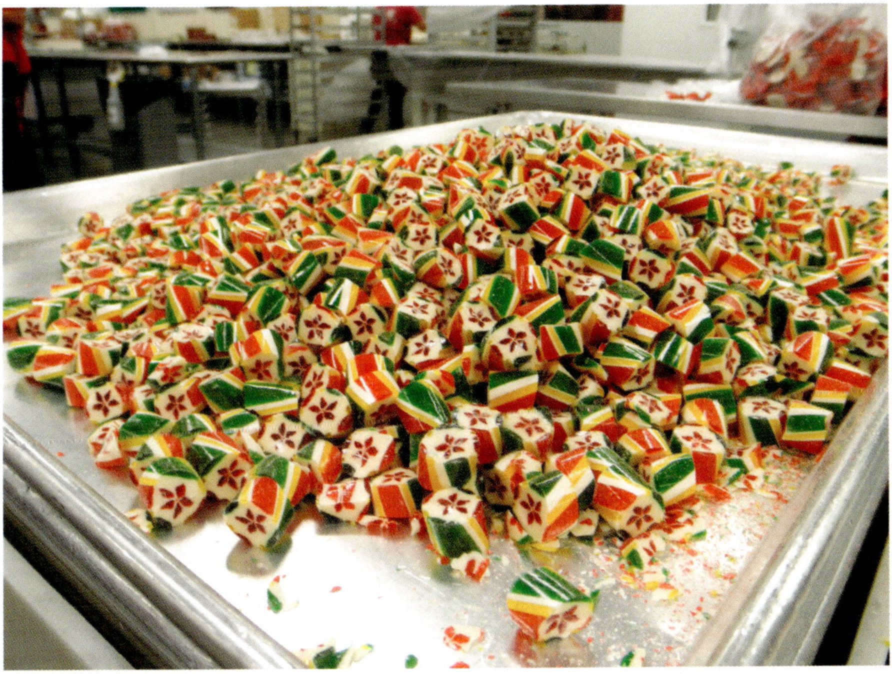

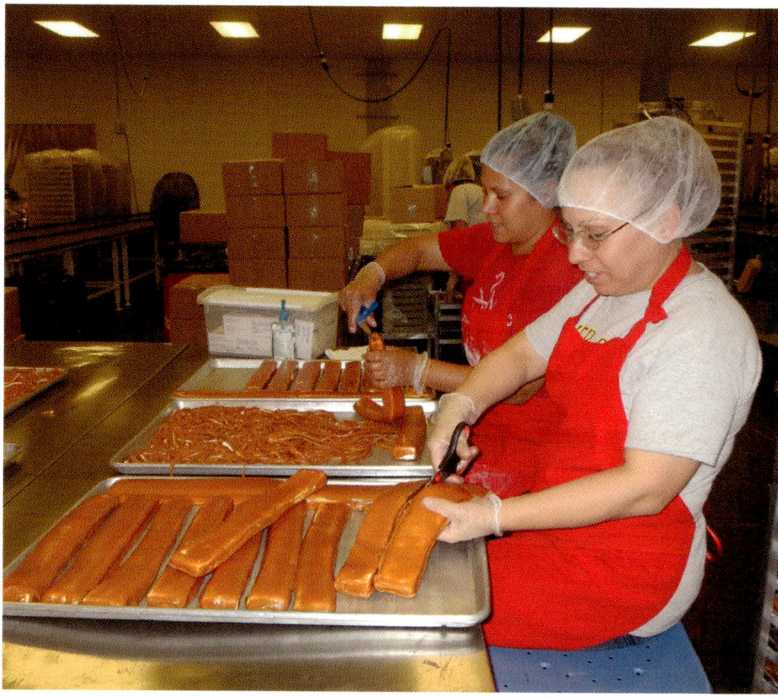

Kitchen assistants cutting the Mitchell Sweets, ending the three-day process of whipping and drying the marshmallow, cooking the caramel and forming the candies. *Photo by the author.*

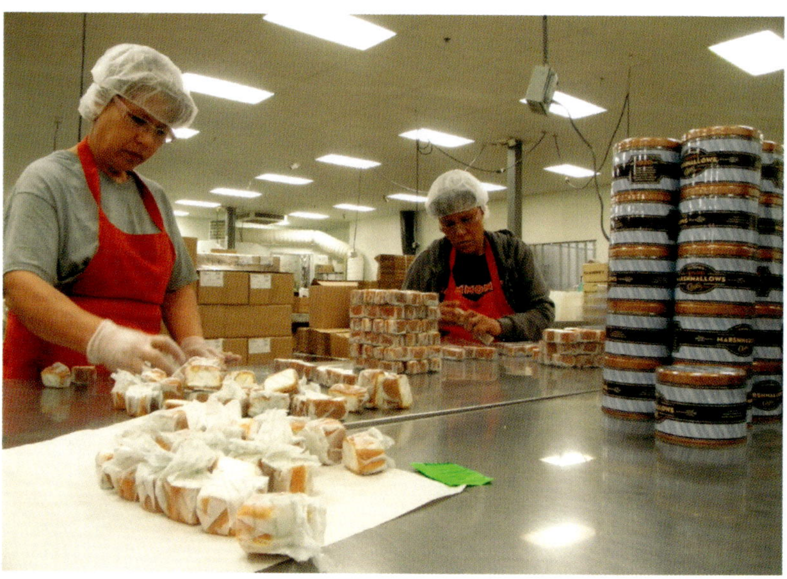

Mitchell Sweets being hand wrapped by a kitchen assistant. *Photo by Michael Scalisi.*

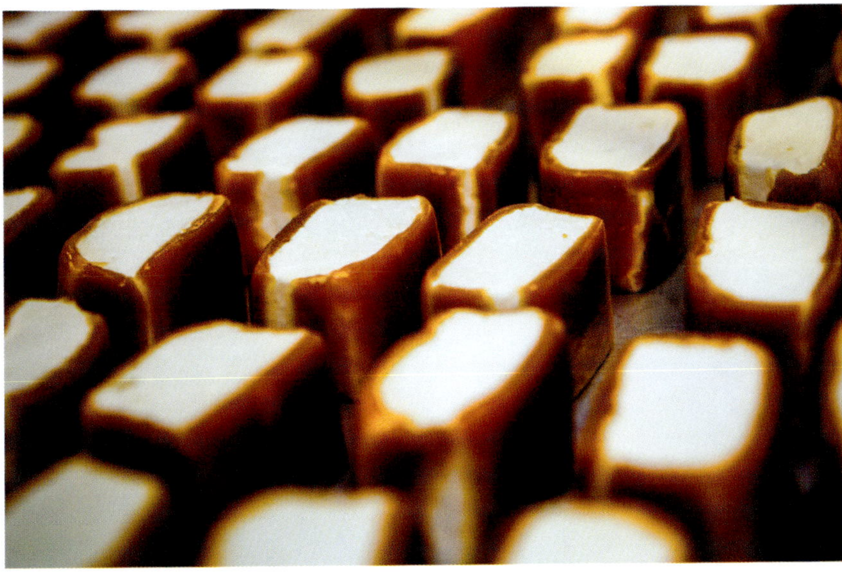

Mitchell Sweets, Hammond's number-one best-selling soft candies since the 1930s. *Photo by McBoat Photography, Centennial, Colorado.*

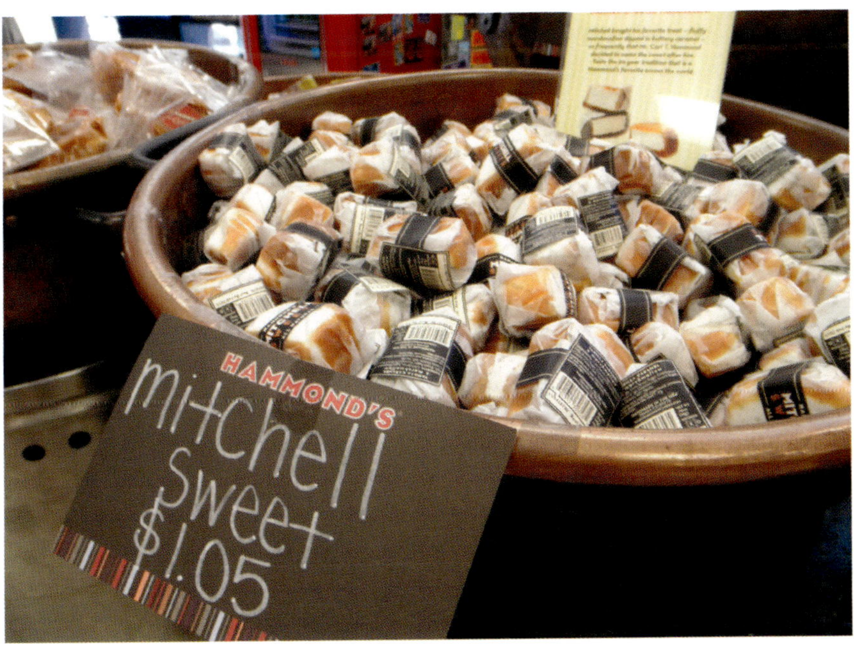

Choosing from the bin of ever-popular Mitchell Sweets enhances any purchase. *Photo by Michael Scalisi.*

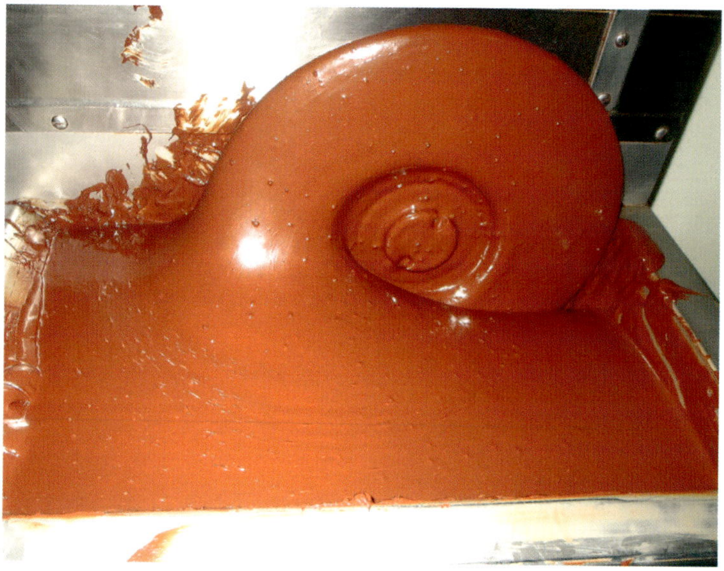

The chocolate tempering machine used for the proper melting, cooling and distribution of cocoa butter in the chocolate. *Photo by the author.*

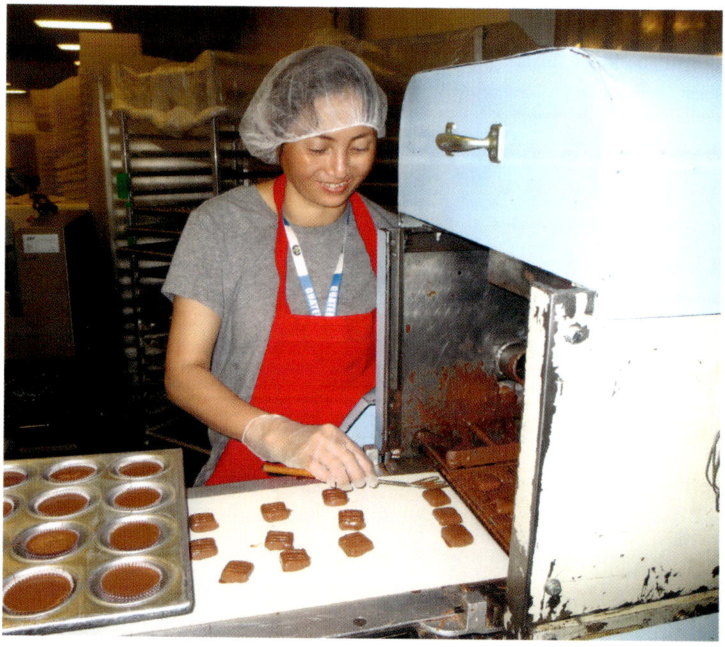

Adding "strings" on individual chocolates to indicate the flavor or filling of the confection. *Photo by the author.*

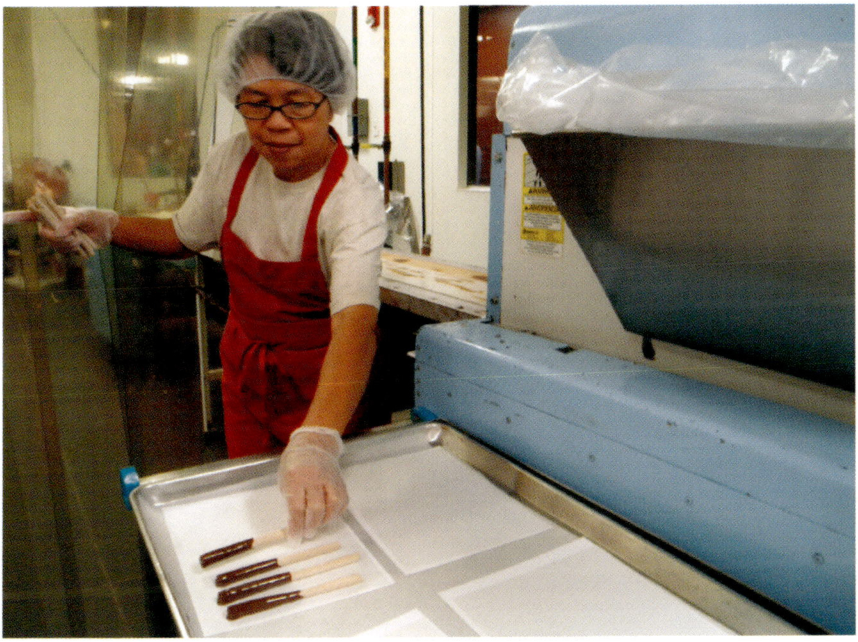

Dipped sticks, one of the many products Hammond's makes for the gourmet food market. *Photo by Michael Scalisi.*

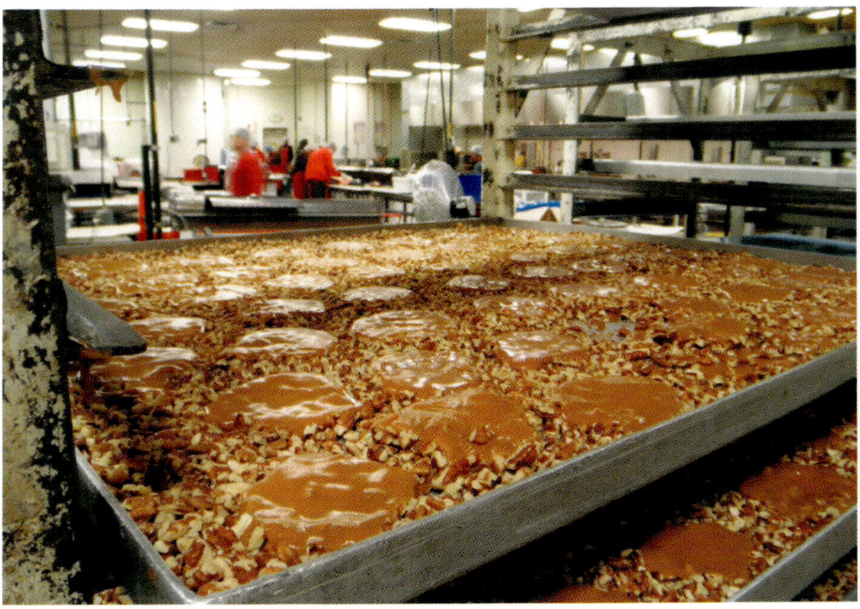

Trays of nutty, caramel Piggy Backs waiting for their chocolate coating. *Photo by Michael Scalisi.*

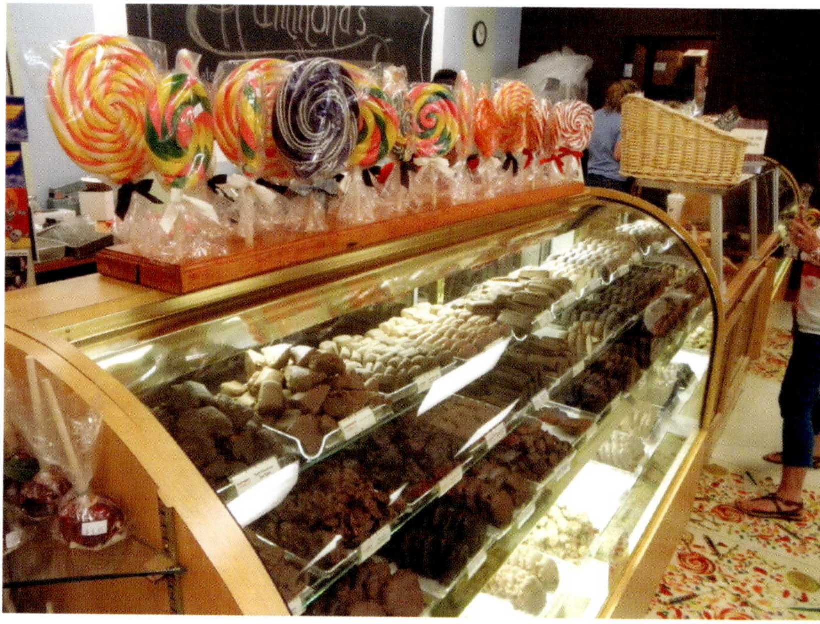

A candy case, reminiscent of Laura Hammond's store, displays the factory's variety of chocolates and fudge delicacies. *Photo by Michael Scalisi.*

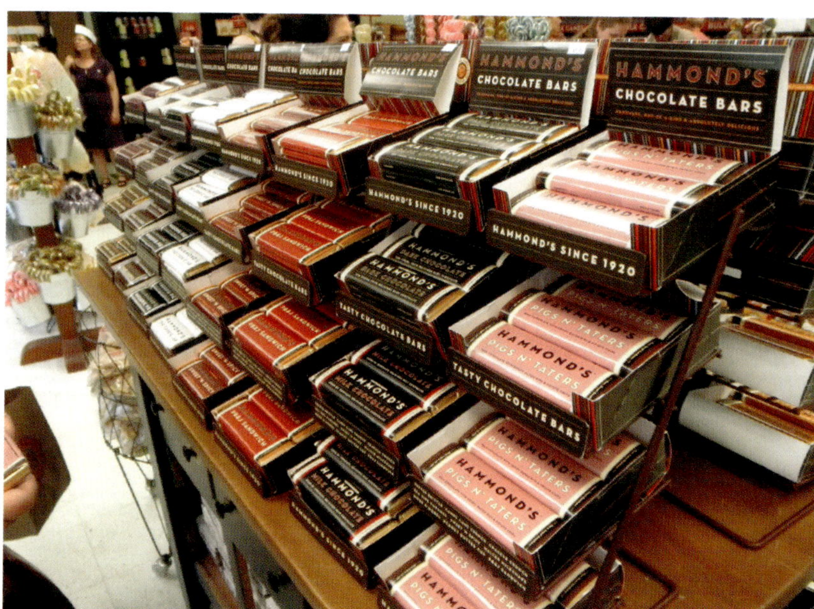

Candy bars, from Candy Cane Crunch to Malted Milkshake, entice buyers. *Photo by Michael Scalisi.*

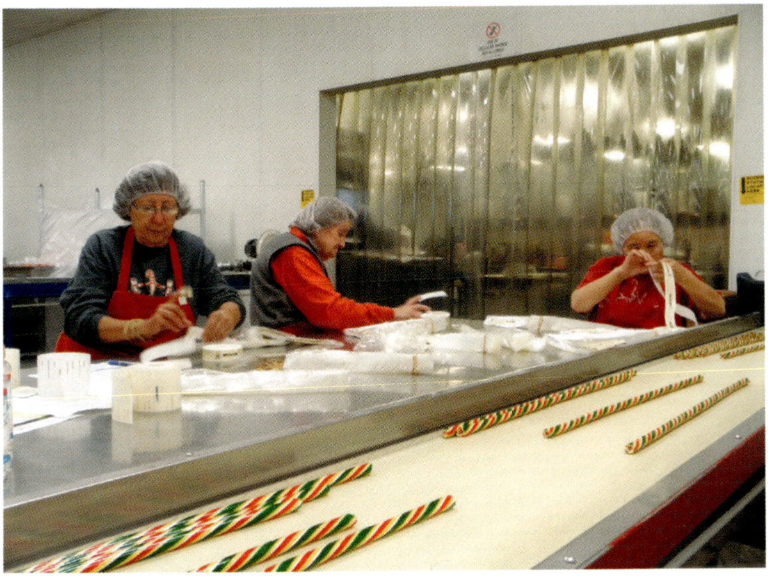

Longtime Hammond's employees labeling sleeve wrappers for the number-one-selling candy canes. *Photo by Michael Scalisi.*

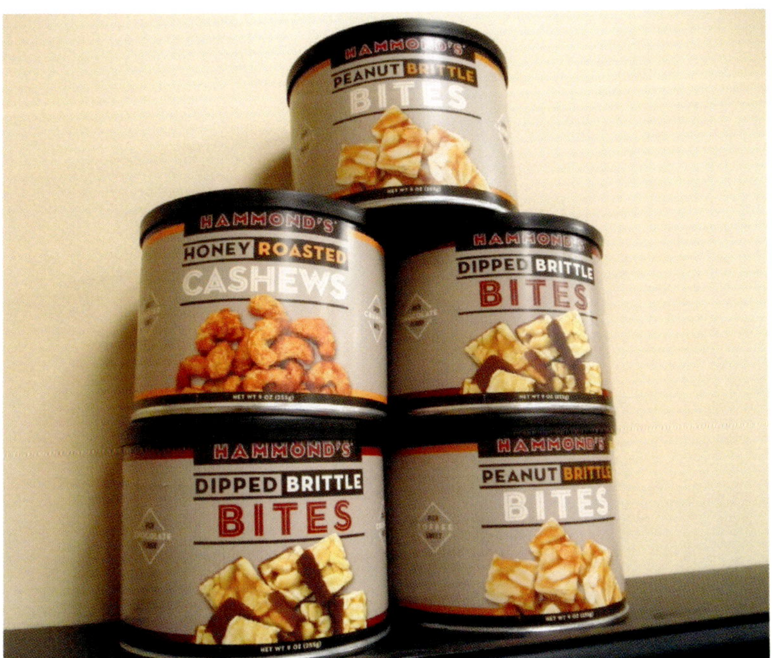

A display of Hammond's varied flavors of brittles and nuts in the factory gift shop. *Photo by Michael Scalisi.*

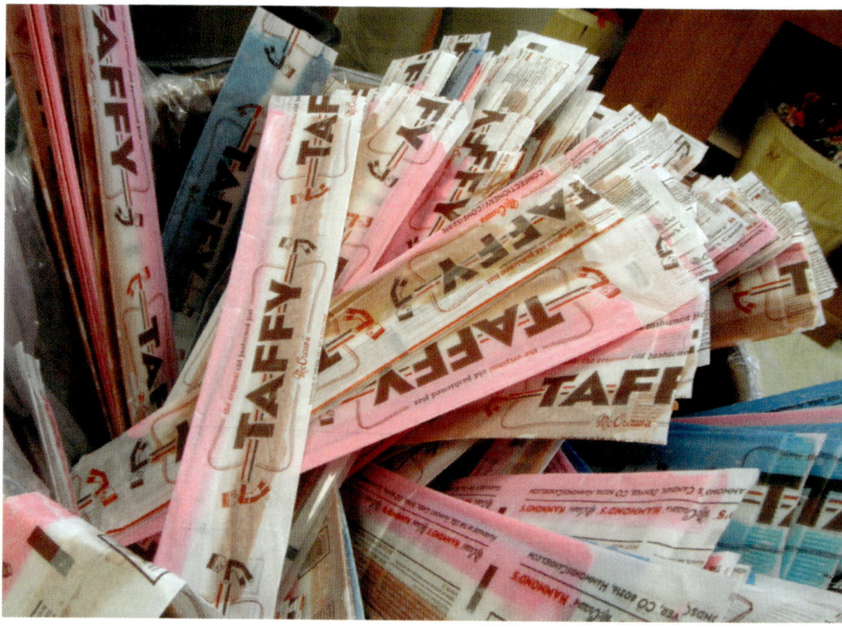

Flat taffy in myriad flavors evokes childhood memories. *Photo by Michael Scalisi.*

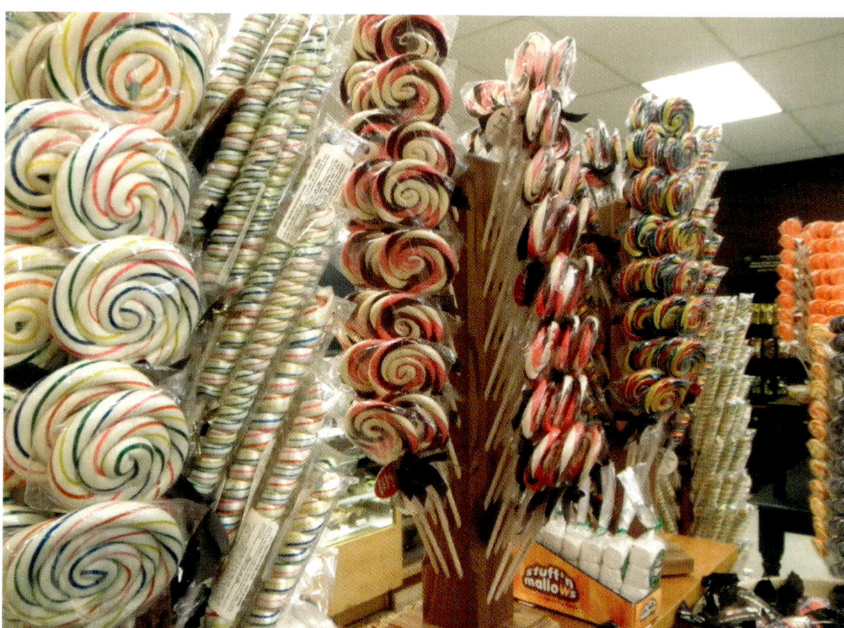

Lollipops in all sizes, shapes and flavors excite the palates of young and old. *Photo by Michael Scalisi.*

Hammond's Candies Product List, circa 1968
Compiled by Carl T. Hammond III

	Hand-Dipped Chocolates	**Type of Chocolate**			
	Soft Centers	Milk	Dark	White*	
1	Chocolate Cream	X	X	X	
2	Vanilla Cream	X	X	X	
3	Maple Cream	X	X	X	
4	Raspberry Cream	X	X	X	
5	Orange Cream	X	X	X	
6	Coconut Cream	X	X	X	
7	Lemon Cream	X	X	X	
8	Jelly	X	X		
9	Fondant Mint Patty	X	X	X	
	Hard Centers	Milk	Dark	White*	
10	Caramel Plain	X	X		
11	Caramel Nut	X	X		
12	Good Jim	X	X		
13	Nougat—Pistachio	X	X		
14	Nougat—Cherry	X	X		
15	Molasses Chip	X	X		
	Clusters	Milk	Dark	White*	
16	Peanut	X	X		
17	Pecan	X	X		
18	Raisin	X			
19	Peppermint Fondant Patty Topped with Peanuts	X			
	Specialty Items	Milk	Dark	White*	
20	Chocolate-Covered Cherries	X	X		
21	Toffee	X			

22	Honey Ko Kos (Hammond's exclusive)	X			
23	Pecan Bark	X	X		
24	Sugar-Free Pecan Bark	X			
25	Peppermint Bark			X	
26	Dipped Dates	X	X		
27	Orange Peel	X	X		
28	Piggy Backs (aka Turtles™)	X	X		
29	Rocky Road (marshmallow and cashews)	X			
	Hand-Cupped Boxed Chocolates	1 lb.	2 lbs.	3 lbs.	5 lbs.
30	Assorted Chocolates (milk/dark/all items)	X	X	X	X
31	All Soft Centers (assorted milk/dark)	X	X		
32	All Hard Centers and Nuts (assorted milk/dark)	X	X		
33	Chocolate-Covered Cherries	X	X		X
34	Toffee Squares	X	X		X
35	Hillman Special (Piggy Backs and Toffee)	X	X	X	X
36	Summer Assortment (White Chocolate)	X			
37	Packed to customer order, any items	X	X	X	X

**White chocolate came in four pastel colors: white, peach, lemon, mint green)*

	BRITTLES	**DESCRIPTION**
38	Peanut Brittle	Traditional peanut brittle
39	Peanut Candy	Peanuts in clear, hard candy coating
40	Cashew Brittle	Cashews in clear, hard candy coating

41	Pecan Brittle	Pecans in clear, hard candy coating
42	All Nut Brittle	Cashews/pecans/walnuts/Brazil nuts
43	Coconut Brittle	Coconut flakes in clear, hard candy coating
44	Peko Flake	Coconut flakes and peanuts in clear
45	Nutty Corn	Popcorn/pecans/cashews/almonds coated with light caramel-butter glaze

	Caramels	**Description**
46	Mitchell Sweets (Hammond's exclusive)	Marshmallow pillows dipped in caramel
47	Plain vanilla	1" cube hand wrapped in cellophane
48	Plain chocolate	1" cube hand wrapped in cellophane
49	Vanilla pecan	1" cube hand wrapped in cellophane
50	Chocolate pecan	1" cube hand wrapped in cellophane
51	Good Jim	Vanilla caramel on roasted almonds
52	Strawberry (flavor)	1"x1.5" hand wrapped in cellophane
53	Licorice (flavor)	1"x1.5" hand wrapped in cellophane

	Fondant Mints		**Fudge**
54	Four shapes matched to wedding colors	70	Chocolate plain
55	Thanksgiving—turkey shaped	71	Chocolate nut (pecans)
56	Christmas—tree shaped	72	Maple plain

57	Christmas—Santa Claus shaped	73	Maple nut (walnuts)
58	Valentine's Day—Heart shaped	74	Divinity (pecans)

	Salt Water Taffy		**Roasted Nuts**
59	County Fair Chews (six flavors)	75	Peanuts
60	Chocolate Pulls (4"x12" slabs)	76	Cashews
61	Strawberry Pulls (4"x12" slabs)	77	Almonds
		78	Bridge mix (five different nuts)

	Hard Candy—Year-Round		**Holiday Candies**
62	Whirl Suckers (three sizes, six flavors)	79	Valentine's Day—hand-dipped
63	Peppermint Pillows (two flavors)		cupped chocolates packed in
64	Barber Polls (four flavors)		heart boxes (six sizes)
65	Horehound Drops	80	Clear candy suckers:
66	Lemon Drops		Halloween (four shapes)
67	Cinnamon Drops		Valentine's Day (heart shaped)
68	Chicken Bones (peanut butter straw dusted with fine coconut)	81	St. Patrick's Day—Divinity
69	Potatoes dusted in cinnamon		

	Hand-Dipped Chocolate Easter Eggs	**Description**
82	Debonnaire: 4-oz. Cream Eggs	Chocolate
83	Debonnaire: 4-oz. Cream Eggs	Vanilla

84	Debonnaire: 4-oz. Cream Eggs	Maple
85	Debonnaire: 4-oz. Cream Eggs	Divinity
86	Debonnaire: 4-oz. Cream Eggs	Cherry Cordial
87	Marshmallow Egg—Milk Chocolate	4" long x 3" wide x 1" thick—egg shaped
88	Banana Marshmallow—Dark Chocolate	4" long x 3" wide x 1" thick—egg shaped
89	8-oz. Cream Eggs—Decorated	Chocolate
90	8-oz. Cream Eggs—Decorated	Vanilla
91	8-oz. Cream Eggs—Decorated	Maple
92	8-oz. Cream Eggs—Decorated	Rocky Road
93	1-lb. Cream Eggs—Decorated	Chocolate
94	1-lb. Cream Eggs—Decorated	Vanilla
95	1-lb. Cream Eggs—Decorated	Rocky Road

	Filled Chocolate Eggs
96	4-oz. jelly beans—4 oz. assorted boxed chocolates
97	8 oz. jelly beans—8 oz. assorted boxed chocolates

	Peak-a-Boo Sugar Eggs
98	Decorated Sugar Eggs Shells filled with visible curios

	Solid Chocolate Easter Figures
99	Hand-molded (six shapes, three sizes)

	Christmas Hard Candy
100	Stain Straws—frosting filled (four flavors)

101	Christmas pillows—nutmeat filled (four flavors)
102	Christmas straws—not filled (two flavors)
103	Christmas pillows—not filled (two flavors)
104	Candy Canes (four sizes—four flavors)
105	Ribbon Candy (two sizes—four flavors)
106	Cut Rock (Art Candy), eight designs

The high quality of Hammond's Candy was ensured not only through its small-batch, handmade production methods but also by not adding preservatives to extend the shelf life. The small batches ensured that any candy purchased at Hammond's had been made within the last couple of weeks and never more than a month before. In addition, the production scheduling was driven by fulfilling the current wholesale orders and then replenishing a base stock of items. So essentially, they made the candy to order, and therefore, it was always fresh.

However, an underlying problem in the candy business during the 1950s and 1960s was that 80 percent of the annual sales were made from Thanksgiving through Easter. And for Hammond's, at least half of the 80 percent was part of the Christmas season. (See chapter nine for the current production schedule.) There were many long hours, including weekends, worked from Halloween through the first week in December.

Most national chocolate confectioners such as See's Candies, Whitman's and Russell Stover could only meet their Christmas demand by producing their chocolates year-round and by adding preservatives and then freezing the finished product. These large manufacturers had sophisticated storage and defrosting methods to ensure that the chocolates purchased over the counter appeared freshly made.

The naturally low humidity in Denver during the fall and winter months made it less likely that the Christmas hard candy would "sweat" and stick together. In addition, all the candy canes were encased in cellophane tubes, the ribbon candy was shrink wrapped and the bulk hard candy was sealed in twenty-five-bag vacuum-pack plastic bags. Even these methods would only ensure their freshness for about thirty days. At Hammond's, the candy was always freshly made. This quality difference allowed the company to compete on a small scale with the big boys.

Fabulous Factory

Although Carl and Harry had built the factory, it seemed that Tom, with his shipboard experience, might have helped to design the efficient use of space. The retail store occupied the front of the building with glass display cases on the three walls opposite the entrance. The cash register was discreetly placed on a counter behind the far case by the doorway to the kitchen and factory. Restrooms were located just beyond that. Carl Sr. had placed his desk opposite that, and the floor safe stood nearby.

There was one unusual object kept in the safe, as illustrated in the following story recounted by Carl III:

The Gun

Nothing is more impressive to a small boy than a gun. There was a gun in the top left-hand drawer of Carl's office desk. It was a small-caliber pistol and looked like the guns in the Dick Tracy Sunday comics. The cylinder was in the floor safe, so the gun was inoperable and safe from the vivid imaginations of kids like me. We were never allowed to touch the gun, let alone play with it. Of course, my grandfather wasn't always at his desk, either. I remember asking Carl why he had a gun, and the answer was so benign that it escapes my memory. He also denied ever needing or using it. It begs the question, why have it in the first place? It makes sense that it was probably a carryover from the Platte Street factory days during the Depression, when Carl worked at night making candy. That probably wasn't the safest place with the railroad terminals and associated warehouses less than a mile away. Certainly there was nothing but candy to steal at the factory at 2550 West Twenty-ninth. The cash register was counted every evening, and the day's cash, with the exception of pennies, was put in the floor safe, which was covered by an inconspicuous rubber mat. Most of the machinery was made from cast iron, and it was the age before computers and electronic equipment. There were never any break-ins that I remember. Occasionally someone would throw a rock at the floor-to-ceiling plate glass windows in the retail store. Eventually, they replaced the glass with unbreakable Plexiglas.

> *Sometime later, however, a classmate told me that the Hammond Candy Factory had made the* CBS Evening News. *During the "happy talk" during the signoff, the anchor mentioned it had been reported that Hammond's Candies had been burglarized. The perpetrator had made off with seven pounds of chocolate-covered cherries and fifty-five pennies.*

The chocolate room—where the temperature was maintained at a chilly fifty-five degrees, making it the only cool part of the space—occupied almost two-thirds of one long wall. One major acquisition that Tom made was the purchase of a chocolate enrober, a device that was particularly useful to coat toffees or clusters. An enrober is a long, narrow mechanism in which the pre-bottomer (aptly named because of the part it plays in the preparation of the confection) coats the bottom of a candy before it goes through the central device where it is completely covered by passing under a curtain of falling melted chocolate. In a factory like Hammond's, there is always a kitchen helper nearby to check the candies, and the enrober in no way replaced the hand dippers. (Today, there are still workers watching the production line to ensure that each piece meets Hammond's standards and that no step in the process is started until the entire operation can be completed.) The dippers' domain was close by the enrober and handily placed near the door that led to the melting tanks for both milk and dark chocolate. The depositor for the creams and the caramel cutter filled the rest of the space. Right outside the chocolate room was the air conditioner and a walk-in cooler for storing the variety of nuts such as peanuts, pecans and walnuts used in making the candy.

Beyond the chocolate room, at the back of the building where temperatures rose to tropical heights, the space was filled with all the equipment and paraphernalia needed to produce the hard candies, canes and lollipops. These included two open-hearth furnaces, a fire mixer and the batch roller, all of which used gas to supply energy and heat and were major contributors to the high temperature. Gas was always used because it is much easier to control in cooking than electricity. That part of the room also contained steel slab tables for coloring and flavoring the hard candies, a marble slab for the fudge and a hardwood table used for cooling. That table had an even more interesting history than the other equipment, which had merely been purchased secondhand. In its earliest form, it had been a bowling lane. Nearby the gigantic corn syrup tank that held one thousand gallons of corn syrup was a large stack of one-hundred-pound bags of sugar, as well as a small table with a scale. Strategically located where it would be available to everyone in the factory was a double sink.

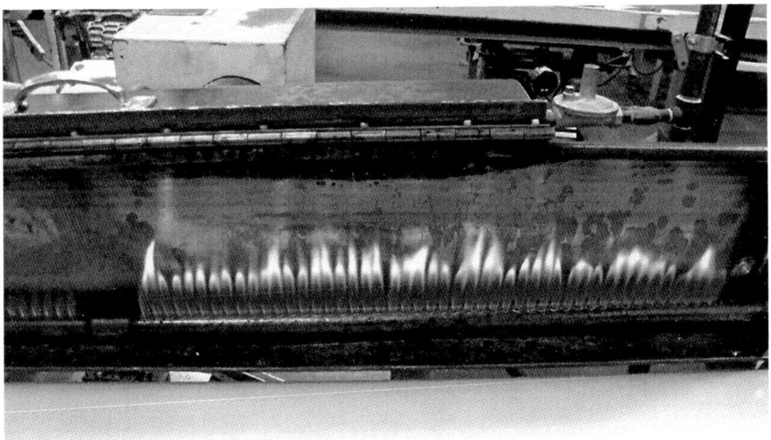

Gas jets on the batch roller contribute to the high temperature of the kitchen. *Photo by the author.*

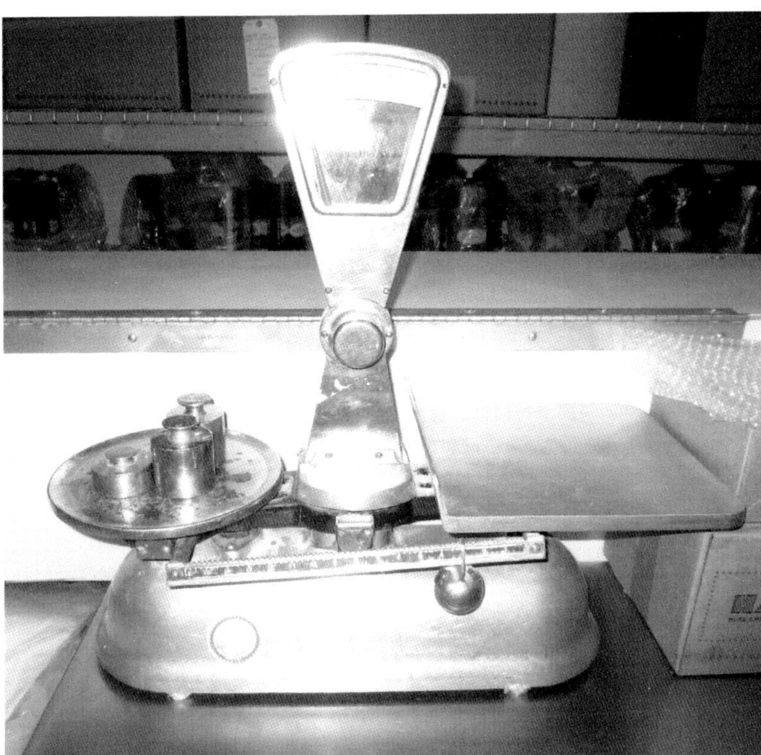

The counter balance scale. *Photo by the author.*

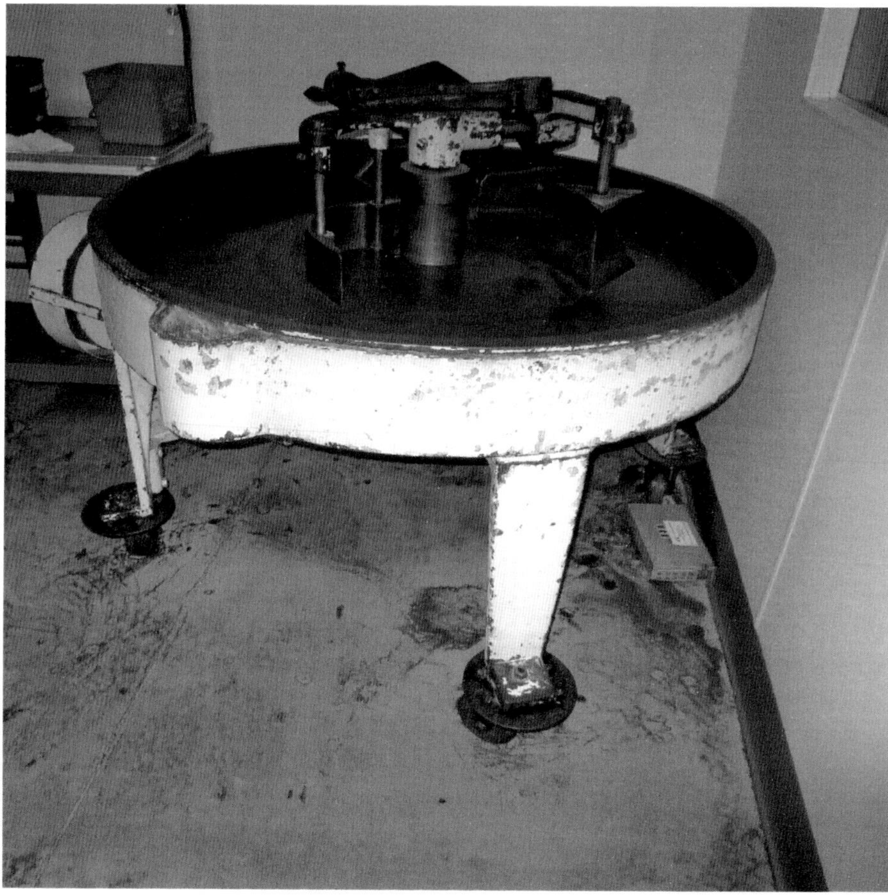

A ball-bearing beater, also called the plow, used for fondant. *Photo by the author.*

Close to one-third of the entire factory space was devoted to several packing tables where most of the candies were sealed, labeled and boxed. If the candy was part of a wholesale order—and during the '50s, 75 percent of it was—the confections would be packaged primarily in fifteen- to twenty-five-pound boxes. The chocolates, however, were placed in five-pound boxes as they came out of the enrober cooling tunnel, exactly like the famous *I Love Lucy* television episode. The five-pound boxes were sold wholesale. Alternatively, one of the helpers would line up an assortment of the five-pound boxes and individually place each piece of chocolate into tiny paper cups as they assembled a retail box of chocolates such as a one-pound box of assorted chocolates.

Near the packing tables, there was also a round mixer, which was imaginatively named the fondant plow, and tucked neatly in between was the table where the very special wedding mints were made. Tom would melt down the fondant and add color to try to match the wedding theme colors. Matching the colors was extremely difficult because most of the time the wedding coordinator would give Tom a piece of fabric to match. Matching the color of candy, which is one medium, to fabric, a different medium, is an arduous task in the best of times and nearly impossible at worst. Additionally, the fondant color will change as it cools. Tom was understandably proud of the fact that he almost always got it right. Tom was a master candy maker in the truest sense of the word.

The Fondant Plow

There is a wonderful story about the several-hundred-pound fondant plow that exemplifies the resilience and ingenuity that is an integral part of any successful business and also illustrates the necessity of self-reliance in an entrepreneur. For some reason, Tom wasn't satisfied with where the machine was standing, and he wanted to move it about ten feet. And so he did. Taking the steel tube that was used for brittle—in a small operation, every implement has multiple uses beyond its original purpose—he placed it on the floor and put a wooden block on either side of the leg. Next he took a long four-foot crowbar with a claw and knob at either end, and slipping the claw under one leg, he then leveraged that off the floor and walked it several inches. He repeated that operation over and over again, leg by leg, and walked it until it was in the spot that suited him. How trite to think, "where there's a will there's a way," but that's how Tom moved the fondant plow all by himself—the Hammond independence in action!

Although one person can lift seventy pounds, it takes two strong candy makers to lift and pour a forty-pound batch of three-hundred-degree candy out of a thirty-pound kettle without someone getting burned. On days when neither Bud DePry nor Tommy Williams was in the factory, Tom had to figure out a way to get the batches poured or production would grind to a halt. No production meant no candy; no candy meant no sales; no sales meant no cash; and no business can survive for long without cash.

Once again, Tom's engineering ingenuity came to the rescue. He installed a J-shaped rail on the ceiling. Hanging from the rail were two chains attached to a winch and a power cord. Tom and another one of the employees would lift the kettle from the furnace onto a circular steel dolly with wheels. Tom would then attach clamps to the chains and kettle handles. Using the power cord, he would winch up the kettle, and the rail would guide the kettle over the steel slab. It was then easy to tip the kettle to pour the molten candy onto the slab. It was a particularly show-stopping solution, and it meant that one of them was then free to pursue another task.

After the small factory on Platte that Carl had used when he started the company, the 2550 location must have seemed very spacious, but in time, Tom took over the space next door at 2530 Twenty-ninth Avenue.

Not So Sharp

Another anecdote illustrates that anyone who tried "sharp business practices" with Tom was woefully ignorant of the character of the man. Because he was essentially a serene person who viewed his world with equanimity, a less scrupulous person, who thought all men were ready to cut corners if it might be worth additional profit, totally misunderstood Tom.

One afternoon, Carl III was back from classes at the University of Denver—he would still work occasionally for his father—when the phone rang. The conversation went like this:

"Oh, really? Are you sure? Oh, I don't think so. Hold on, he's right here." Balancing the receiver on his shoulder so the person on the other end of the line couldn't hear him, Tom called over to his son, "Hey, Carl, did you deliver three fifteen-pound cases of brittle to that company yesterday?"

Carl affirmed he had surely done so.

"Yes, he delivered it." A noise like static ensued. "No, we're not going to deliver another one. Really? Well, I'm holding a signed invoice for three cases right here in my hand. Sure, we can send another case, but you will be invoiced. OK, we'll wait to hear back." Uncharacteristically, Tom hung up the phone a little harder than usual.

"Maybe they misplaced it," young Carl offered.

"I doubt it," said his father. "They probably just wanted another case for free to lower their overall cost. They thought if they said we shorted them, we'd give them another for free to ensure future business with them."

"Do you think they will order more?"

"Probably not, but that's OK. Once you start down that road, they'll just keep asking for more until you say no."

Fundraising

Local organizations or schools knew, however, that Hammond's would assist them in their fundraising events, selling to them at wholesale prices, and children were often seen lugging boxes of candy bars or hard candies from door to door. The lucky ones had younger brothers or sisters to loan them their red Radio Flyer wagons to haul up and down the North Denver hills. A young salesperson was even more fortunate if he could borrow one of the flyers with the wood slatted sides; not only could they hold more boxes, but if they zealously piled up too many packages, there was much less chance they would roll back down a hill.

Gini Benvenuti, who graduated from North High School in the 1950s and grew up in a family active in the Masons, was a devoted member of Job's Daughters. First elected as an officer in the organization, she was next voted to be the "Honored Queen," whose responsibility was to run the annual fund program. She was also able to choose how to raise the monies. Gini recalls selling one-pound boxes of candy and five-pound boxes of canes with such a success rate that they exceeded Hammond's original allocation. The company generously provided more. Gini's fond memories of shopping in the store include gazing wistfully through the fronts of the clear glass cases, wishing she didn't have to make a choice but finally making a decision. Like many a shopper before and after, she pronounced the Mitchell Sweets "sooo good." "They were wonderful," she still enthuses.

Once, when she and her fellow Job's Daughters stopped to pick up some more candy, they were invited to take a behind-the-scenes tour of the factory, an event they bragged about at their next meeting. Normally, they could just see into the factory through the doorway, and she still describes seeing the workers operate the candy puller in the back. They were sometimes still using the hook that Carl had installed in his first store if they were working on small lots to add many different colors to a batch. They could only use the puller for large twenty- or thirty-pound blocks, so it was practical to keep the hook for when they were working with smaller, five-pound amounts.

HARD CANDY HEAVEN

"It wasn't Christmas without Hammond's Candies," says Research Librarian James Jeffrey of the Western History and Genealogy Department at the Denver Public Library. He especially remembers the colorful round tins of ribbon candy and the hard mix that had to be kept tightly closed because, as Tom Hammond remarked to a reporter visiting the factory, "it will keep forever if you keep it away from moisture. Sugar is a preservative. At 320 degrees, we burned all the moisture out. On a damp day, the candy will grab moisture right out of the air if you give it a chance."[54]

In those days, Hammond Candies went through 2,000 to 2,500 pounds of hard mix and 1,000 to 1,200 pounds of ribbon candy during the holiday season, but the heaviest demand year round was for the chocolates—the Honey Ko Kos the founder originated and the Swiss mints. Tom boasted that the aroma of cinnamon the visitors could smell was the pure spice that cost forty dollars a pound[55] (about $154 today).[56]

He reminisced about how his father's satin mix—"the deluxe of hard candies with a vivid hard jacket around a nut or cream center"—had been a big favorite in the old days. "But now sales are dropping off because not enough people know what it is. If you don't have wide distribution, who's going to know what you've got? Firms back east put out a satin mix but they have mass production and they don't use frosting or nut-paste in the center so, it gets hard. It's nothing like the same product."[57]

Then Marie Negri took over, explaining the precision needed to carefully align the curly strips for packing: "The strips have to be exactly ten inches to fit the boxes. The package is more expensive than the candy but there's no way to keep it from breaking otherwise. We have to sell it by the pound package."[58]

Tom became almost prophetic about what would happen many years later when he expressed the hope that the new interest in food specialty shops and handmade things meant a renewed interest in the kinds of products only Hammond's could offer. "If you look around, up until now people have been taking too much for granted about the things they ate. They didn't much care about how something tasted or what quality it was. They were judging more by what something cost than what quality it was. Now it looks as though some people are starting to care again."[59]

Another memory from the family storyteller reflects Tom's philosophy as well as the scarcity of handmade hard candy. He was delivering an order to a specialty shop when he saw that it was selling candy canes for two dollars

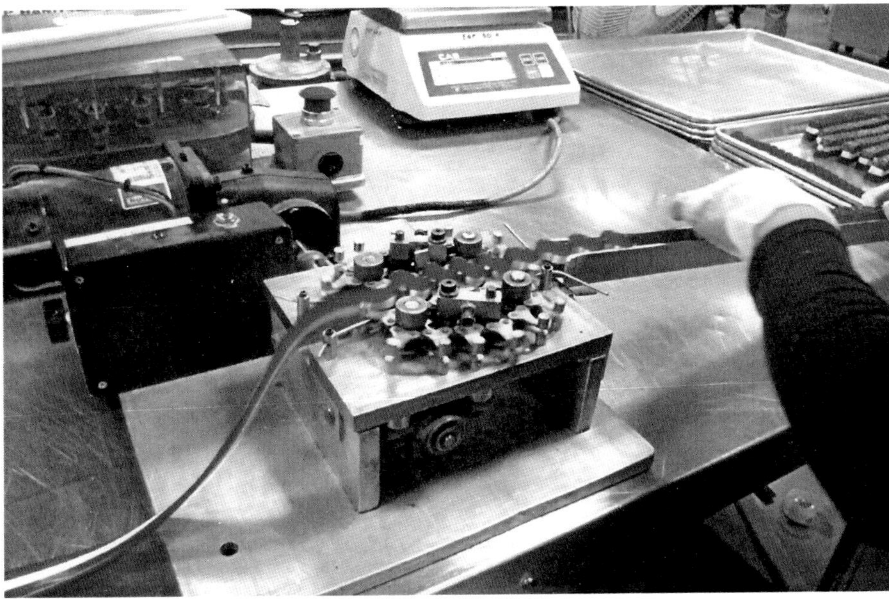

The ribbon candy machine, once hand cranked, now has a small motor, but the candy is still hand fed and cut after it is crimped. *Photo by the author.*

each. "They are yucky looking," he related to his father when he finished his rounds. "You're selling yours for thirty-five cents. You could raise your price to seventy-five cents, they would mark them even higher and we'd both make a profit."

"You still don't understand," his father replied. "I'm doing what I love, and I'm happy with my living."

In reality, it seems fortuitous that circumstances forced Tom to discontinue his studies at the mining school, since he was so content with his life as a candy maker.

He emphasized that fact even more when his mother died. Curiously, the *Denver Post* published an article that detailed the extent of her estate as well as its directives. Laura had left everything of her almost $360,000 assets, except for the candy factory, to her daughter, Marjorie Lutz.[60] June, Tom's wife, told one of her sons how this really upset her and then added, "But your dad just said, 'Don't worry about it. Marge can have all of that; I'm the lucky one because my mother left me the candy factory and now we have a chance to make a living.' I sure admire your dad! He doesn't spend any time with negative thoughts. I wish I could do that."

Feel and Touch

Bud DePry, who was another master and old hand at candy making, joined Hammond's in about 1970. He had started in the business when he was fourteen years old and had tried to start a candy company at one time. When he contacted Tom, he probably didn't even know that Carl, whom he had known in prior years, had died. DePry had been on reserve and active duty with the U.S. Army Air Corps and Colorado Air National Guard until his retirement in 1965, but he got tired of inaction and joined Hammond's. He worked on Mondays and Fridays, when hard candy was made. He became one of Hammond's greatest treasures.

In addition to adding an industry expert in confections, Tom was bringing on a colleague with whom he could share questions and problems. If the pre-enrober's motor slowed down or the fondant plow got clogged, he knew that the production of lollipops would still continue and the rock candy would take shape while he tinkered with the defective tool. The upside of being one's own man in a small operation was the same as the downside—you were still the only person available to make the decisions and, in many cases, to make the repairs.

June recounted a situation when even her usually cool husband lost his composure. It happened that a machine went on the blink just when her pastor had chosen to call and was in the back admiring Tom's candy making. While the kitchen helpers had to keep fifty pounds of candy warm while the equipment was being repaired, June said Tom was using descriptions hardly as sweet as his product. The minister quickly scurried through to the front of the shop, where retail candy is sold, and observed to June, "I don't think Tom is very happy back there."[61]

"But there are rewards when things go well. I enjoy it," said DePry. "It's hard work, but self-satisfying producing something that looks nice."[62] Depry's ability to pick up the knack of candy making so readily when he returned showed what everyone recognizes about confectionary talents—it's all done by feel and touch. Others say simply, "You know it if you do it."

On one point Carl and Bud would have disagreed, and that was what to do with the scrap candy. In many batches of hard candy there are some—particularly the ends of the blocks as they are manipulated and pulled before they are cut to size—that just don't measure up to the desired quality. Bud would keep them aside so that they could be remelted and added to a subsequent lot where the flavor would be cooked off if necessary. Carl preferred to sell them in five-cent scrap bags—that was a boon for customers during the Depression, and when they moved to Twenty-ninth Avenue, it was much favored by the children who could come in the afternoon from the Ashland School across the street, now the site of the Jose Valdez Elementary School.

GENERATION GAP

It isn't always possible to bridge the generational gap, as Carl III learned one day when he tried to change Tom's accounting methods. One of the foundations of any successful business is cost accounting, knowing how much it costs to produce your product.

Cost accounting at Hammond's involved a stack of handwritten three- by five-inch cards, one for each product, which listed the amount of ingredients with their associated costs and the labor time required with the associated wage rate. These material and labor costs were then doubled. The wholesale and retail selling prices of the product were driven by the total cost.

Carl III asked Tom, "Why do you double the cost?"

"Oh," he said, "that's for everything else."

"Like what?"

"You know, like the lights and everything."

Then Carl III asked, "What happens when prices change, like the cost of peanuts or chocolate?"

Tom replied, "Well, if it is a big change, I go back and recalculate all the affected cards. If it is not a big change, I just adjust the price."

Carl III refrained from asking what his dad meant by big change. Being a senior-year accounting major at the University of Denver at the time, he wasn't impressed with Tom's cost accounting acumen. So he designed a cost accounting system for the Hammond Candy Co. as a special project for his cost accounting class. It would allow him to continually monitor and update the product costs and more accurately calculate the "everything else," which in cost accounting parlance is "overhead." In theory, this would allow for a more accurate pricing. He showed it to Tom.

"OK," he asked. "How many people would it take to maintain this cost accounting?"

"Probably one person working half-time," Carl III replied.

"Can I increase the price of the candy to pay for this person?"

Uh-oh. "Probably not," Carl III had to admit.

"Can't use it. Sorry."

"Oh well," Carl III consoled himself. He got an A+ on the project.

Even though they might not have always followed their offspring's suggestions, Tom and June continued the family pattern of encouraging the kind of independence that allowed them to follow their own paths. Although it might have pained Tom that none of his children wanted to model their careers on his or their grandfather's, he never admitted it. Carl III came back into the business briefly in 1983 (see chapter seven) during a break in his accounting career and then returned to San Diego. George chose the military for his initial career after graduating from the University of Northern Colorado and upon retirement from the U.S. Air Force earned his master's degree in basic science at the University of Colorado at Denver. He then taught physics and astronomy at his alma mater for some ten years.

Keith enlisted in the U.S. Navy during the Vietnam War to see the world, but they made him a medic, and he ended up spending four years stationed at navy hospitals in Southern California. He was a fortunate man; many of his buddies were sent to Vietnam, where the survival rate of medics was less than 20 percent. Keith finished his education at the University of Colorado in chemistry and subsequently worked in the oil industry.

Patrick followed his dad's ambition, attending the Colorado School of Mines and moving to Minnesota upon graduation to pursue a career in operations research. Robin came closest to it through Emery, her husband, although she herself chose a medical field, graduated from the University of Colorado at Denver and became a phlebotomist. Tom invited her husband, Emery Dorsey, to come to work at Hammond's in 1981. Emery took over the family helm after Tom's passing in 1985.

Chapter 7

Third-Generation Candy Maker

New Beginnings

Robin Hammond, Tom and June's daughter, married Emery Dorsey in 1978 and moved to Fort Collins, Colorado, until he graduated from Colorado State University. During the semester breaks, Emery worked at Hammond's, where his considerable brawn was put to the test moving the sugar and stacking the one-hundred-pound bags. Since each batch of candy requires about twenty pounds of sugar and another fifteen pounds of corn syrup cooked in a thirty-pound copper kettle, strength and agility are positive features. At that time, he had no intention of making candy his life's work, although his own family had a history of involvement in the food industry. On Emery's current website for Nostalgic Confections, he refers to the "spirit of the confectionery arts and the unwavering belief in the joy of food," but it seems that during his first job at Hammond's, he may have been unaware that he had an inborn attraction to the industry.

After they returned to Denver, Robin worked and went to school while Emery worked in a family business called the Fruit Basket, which his grandfather had started during the 1930s. At about the same time, he also worked part time at Hammond's through 1984, when he became a full-time employee.

In the summer of 1983, as Emery was deciding on whether to pursue a career with the Fruit Basket or Hammond's, his brother-in-law Carl III decided to move his wife, Jo Anne, and their two boys back to Denver. Carl III had just completed twelve successful years as a CPA and financial executive. He planned to start a catalogue business featuring several of the more popular Hammond's Candies items. Within a year, they were back in San Diego, not because they hadn't received enough orders but because Hammond's couldn't make enough candy.

The four-color catalogue Carl III produced was full of mouthwatering photos such as caramel being poured out of a copper kettle onto a bed of pecans, and the elegant cover featured foil-wrapped candies in a Waterford compote. The catalogue was aimed directly at the profitable retail market. Unfortunately, the retail sales from the catalogue were modest; however, the wholesale sales from other retailers who saw the catalogue were substantial.

The largest wholesale order came from Sid's Market, a precursor to today's upscale specialty retail markets. Sid's had been a large Hammond's customer for about three years and, based on the slick-back catalogue, tripled its order for 1983. Carl III's venture was going to be a success. However, a fateful call intervened the week after Thanksgiving, when a disastrous fire destroyed the shopping center where Sid's was located. The customer cancelled its entire order. It turned out to be a blessing in disguise for Hammond's.

Just three days earlier, Tom had announced to Carl III that he had completed almost all the hard candy assortments with the exception of twenty more batches of canes. His son hadn't had the heart to tell him that Sid's order alone would require half again as much production. It was clear that Tom did not have the capacity to meet the demand Carl III's catalogue had created. But Carl III knew on an emotional level that he couldn't go to his dad and say it was time to change the business model. That would have entailed mortgaging the factory and maybe Tom's house. Additionally, it would have required Hammond's to double its employees. Carl III knew his dad had never borrowed a dime in his life, and Carl III couldn't ask his dad to risk his life's work on a roll of the dice.

Tom was always more comfortable as a small businessman, and he preferred to run his company in much the same way as his father had. For example, Hammond's had never seen any reason to advertise and certainly had never felt the need for a catalogue; they believed they had achieved success because they had never overreached what they could do. Both Tom and his father believed they needed only one place to make and sell their candy. Opening other sites would mean paying rent, and that would lead to borrowing and debt. Such a situation was totally against Carl's philosophy, and Tom had learned well from him. It was, to some extent, a credo shared by many who had struggled through the Depression years.

It is probable that at times Tom chafed under Carl's stringent methods but accepted his inability to change; in the same way, Carl III understood that Tom couldn't grasp the magnitude of his business proposal. But each respected his father too much to quibble, so Carl III and Jo Anne moved back to San Diego, where he successfully resurrected his accounting career. He never regretted his time in Denver, as it gave him the opportunity to work with his father as a colleague instead of just a son.

Still Another Era

Six months after relocating to San Diego, Carl III got another fateful call, this time from his mother: "Oh, Carl, your dad just had a massive heart attack. He was here eating lunch…he's gone."

In a less closely knit family where responsibilities are taken more lightly, the sudden death of the family business leader who has left no succession plan frequently means that the company itself may be breathing its last. However, when June asked Emery Dorsey to step up and take over, he graciously assented. Anyone who knows candy and has had any connection with Hammond's from that time states unequivocally that Emery saved the business; in fact, they will add that he also raised it to another level.

Emery explains his success in another way, saying:

> *I didn't save the business; I just happened to be around when my father-in-law passed away. They had focused much of their attention on training and apprenticeship before he died, but Dad left with a lot of the knowledge he had with him. Dad was great at soft candy and chocolate and was good at hard candy too. Bud DePry, Tommy Williams and Tommy Job helped a lot even though they were retired and had just helped Dad part time. There were friends that also helped. Mom* [June] *was very supportive. I have to admit that it was a lesson in apprenticeship, self-determination and my inner comprehension and understanding, which Dad used to say was hard to find.*

Despite Emery's protestations, there is general agreement that without Emery, there would be no Hammond's today.

When Emery began full time at Hammond's, it was a perfect time for someone aspiring to learn the skills needed in handmade candy production. Master candy maker Bud DePry, veteran caramel expert Tommy Williams and their assistant, Tommy Job, delighted in welcoming a recruit who was genuinely interested in learning their craft. Bud introduced him to the art of making cut rock, the most difficult, intricate and beautiful of all hard candies. (This would be important in the later development of the company.) What young children haven't thrilled to their first sight and taste of a perfectly shaped round delight centered with a picture of a star, a flower, Santa Claus or a witch? Only the most dexterous of the cut rock makers can aspire to creating an anchor and chain or crossed flags on a pole, but the teachers were there to instruct Emery and to keep their artistry alive.

Williams, the caramel man whom Tom had so generously welcomed back after his unfortunate experience with the other company, and Tommy Job patiently taught Emery what they knew. Job would continue to work there into the 1990s when he himself was over eighty years old. A former salesman, like many men who had lived through the Great Depression, he simply derived great satisfaction from having something that kept him busy and valued. As mentors, they could pass on not only the tips of the trade and the ways to develop his artistic talent but also how to understand when the candy was ready, to get to know by the feel. Seasoned practitioners say no one becomes proficient until he makes one thousand pounds or ten thousand canes. Anxious to learn more about chocolate, Emery had only to look to another candy artist, John Pulsit, for instruction. Commenting on his colleagues, Emery remarks, "Dad hired all retired folks to work for him. Mickey (who started in 1982) and I were the youngest there. It was an older crowd, very interesting."

Although many of the other workers were considerably older, Tom was chronologically still relatively young, just sixty-three years old, at the time of his death. But his long hours of work every day for so many years had taken their toll, and he looked old beyond his years in the pictures taken for the newspapers in the '70s. Perhaps, as someone raised with Christian Science beliefs, he had disregarded his aches and pains or overlooked them.

Tom had become a fixture in his community, a man esteemed for his business practices, appreciated for his generosity and valued for his friendship and integrity. There was standing room only at his funeral. "Dad was a good candy maker but a really great person. He would take time to talk to customers, friends in the business—he was truly loved and admired," his son-in-law, Emery Dorsey, says even now. (See the appendix to read the eulogy given by his son Carl III.)

National News

If Tom had found his son and son-in-law's occasional murmurs about expansion bewildering, he would surely have shaken his head at the changes that occurred in the latter part of the '80s and into the next decade. Emery had become a brilliant candy maker. Like Carl and Tom, he became proficient with all kinds—chocolates, brittles, caramels and Hammond's greatest asset, hard candies. It seemed the news was spreading throughout the trade, and before long, Harry and David's was knocking on their door, anxious to add the ribbon candy to its line of products. That company even designed a special kind of tin so that those most fragile of candies could be safely transported over long distances, thus solving a problem that had plagued Tom years before. It was a boon to the business, but it meant Emery put in grueling hours, an almost superhuman kind of schedule a person might take upon himself but could never ask of an employee. During one year, he was working seven days a week, ten to twelve hours on weekdays and giving himself a bit of a break on the weekends, when he cut his day by a couple of hours. He admits today, "I believe that the time on the hard floor, in front of the heat and the amount of hours aged me a bit. I am glad I was a big, strong person." He was also smart, hiring a marketer and prevailing upon his mother-in-law for financial as well as moral support when it was necessary. She was thrilled to help and be a part of his achievements.

In 1994, *Saveur*, an elegant magazine of haute cuisine and glamorous photography, sent a writer and the photographer Dominique Vorillon to Hammond's to interview Emery and photograph him and June in the kitchens. The November issue featured an article, "Christmas in the Candy Factory," and life at Hammond's changed forever. Williams-Sonoma gave its first order of toffee, establishing a tie that lasted for years, and there were features on PBS and the Food Channel and the chance to participate in a Smithsonian Institution program. The number of full-time employees increased, and Emery hired a lot of part-time people from the high schools.

Like his father-in-law, Emery inspired loyalty and the ability to develop relationships within the staff. "I do miss the fact that we all considered ourselves family. It was an indescribable experience," he still remembers after all these years. But it is another statement that shows he still reflected Carl Sr.'s ideas: "From a personal perspective, what gives me the most joy and pride is the ability to maintain the traditions that have become part of the fabric of individuals and families here in Denver and across the country. Being part of the experience is very moving and often humbling, such as watching children whose eyes light up when they get an old-fashioned lollipop or candy cane."

Emery also understood the elder Hammond's thinking:

> *This I know is true. I think as young adults we all have visions and dream of building something big and wonderful. Dad missed that opportunity a bit with his service in World War II. Carl had his opportunity with the Old Dutch Mill off Speer. Carl III had his plans with his move back to Denver and the hopeful expansion. By the time he came back, Dad did not fully realize the amount of work, production and cost that was in Carl III's vision. It was a bit of a difficult period. I ran my dreams through Hammond's as well; funny, looking back, I would embrace that small business concept now in a heartbeat.*

Describing his short time with Tom, he adds, "It was a great learning environment. Still run much like I envisioned it running in the 1930s and '40s. I have to admit I fell in love with it, even though it was difficult."

Much as Emery appreciated the value of all that had been handed down throughout two generations, he also wanted to build on that foundation. For him, that meant adding to the visibility of the company by opening other retail facilities. He achieved that when he contracted with Sandy Gerger at Elitch Gardens to market Hammond's candies at the ever-popular theme park. His idea that candy and amusement rides were a selling combination proved to be correct, but unfortunately, Elitch's moved to its present location only three years later. The increase in rents made it unprofitable to continue this venture. Emery also opened a similar operation in the old Tivoli Brewing Company shopping area, but that closed when June sold it at the end of the 1990s.

After Tom's death, June continued to be a familiar face at North Denver events and enjoyed having her sons accompany her. One afternoon, she and Carl III were at a function run by the Shriners when an old-time acquaintance excused herself, saying, "I'm sorry, I have to leave now. I'm driving up to Estes Park to buy the best toffee I've ever tasted."

"Oh, really?" asked June. "Where do you get it?" Upon hearing the answer, June smiled at her friend and responded, "Well, I'll be able to save you a four-hour trip. That's Hammond's toffee, and you can just go over to 2550 Twenty-ninth Avenue to buy it." The Hammond family also have a favorite recipe for their own home use.

A HAMMOND FAMILY HOME-STYLE CANDY RECIPE

Carl T. Hammond III Family Collection

Almond Toffee

Tools:

large nonstick sauce pan
wooden spoon or high-temp rubber spatula
metal spatula
cookie pans with edges
thermometer
large coating bowls or surfaces
scale

Ingredients:	cups	oz.	lbs.
butter	3.75	30	1.875
sugar	4.125	33	2.0625
salt		pinch	to taste
lecithin	1 tsp.	0.5	1 tsp.
raw ground almonds	1.5	12	0.75

- *Melt butter and add sugar, salt and lecithin in a large nonstick sauce pan.*
- *Cook over medium heat, stir frequently and watch for scorching.*
- *Add almonds at 250 degrees, stir constantly at a slow consistent pace (don't stir fast or sugar and butter will separate).*
- *Cook to 300 degrees or until golden in color;* **don't overcook.**
- *Carefully pour on lightly greased sheet pans with edges to desired thickness.*
- *Spread with a knife, spoon or metal spatula (don't overspread).*
- *Thinner toffee will cool quicker, eat better and may not bleed off a lot of butter.*
- *Let cool and carefully flip over.*
- *Mixture is very hot and can severely burn. BE CAREFUL! If there is a lot of residual butter, blot with paper towel.*
- *Allow to completely cool and break into larger pieces.*

Chocolate:

- *Melt chocolate of choice in microwave or double boiler. Do not exceed 120 degrees.*
- *Dip toffee in chocolate at about 100 degrees.*
- *Hand dip, covering all sides of toffee.*
- *Set in ground almonds and coat.*
- *Place on tray or pan and let dry.*

Almonds for topping:

Ingredients:	cups	oz.	lbs.
Almonds	4	32	2

- *It's OK to use raw or roasted almonds. You can dry roast them in the oven or grease roast on the stove. The simple method is to purchase roasted almonds from the store.*
- *Grind to desired texture in a food processor; finely ground almonds mixed with medium-fine coat the toffee better.*
- *Almonds should be cool when dipping toffee.*
- *Store in an airtight container.*

A YOUTHFUL VIEW

Now that she was on her own, June exhibited a flair for managing her own affairs and became more active in the workings of the factory. Carl III attributed her financial sense to lessons she had learned growing up when her family had suffered economic setbacks. Her father, Martin "Doc" Jones, was a contractor who moved his family from Los Angeles to Escalon, California, when he lost everything in the Great Depression. Doc and his wife, Edna, had moved from Joplin, Missouri, to Los Angeles, where he successfully built roads using twenty mule teams. Starting from scratch again in Escalon, he began farming with peaches and pecans while he built barns, along with other construction work, as it came up. His business sense was lacking, though, and when he died sometime in the 1950s, everyone in the town of Escalon owed him money. Carl III thinks that hardened his mother, who determined that would never happen to her, and it gave her the business acumen to successfully support Emery's ambitions to grow the company.

Unlike Tom, Carl III says June appeared twenty years younger than she actually was. During the 1980s, he went to a brunch with her and ran into friends who hadn't seen him in a long time. At first not recognizing him, the former neighbor then tactlessly remarked, "You look older than your mother." Fortunately, Carl III inherited Tom's sense not to take oneself too seriously, and he simply laughed out loud. When he was serving himself at the buffet table, he heard voices from the kitchen: "I thought that he was her husband, not her son."

Such mistakes didn't end there. Several years later, June, then in her eighties, went to California for her brother's funeral and began bantering with the woman at the hotel desk. "If we don't like this room, then we're not going to take it," she was saying, when the woman playfully interrupted, "Then you and your husband…"

"That's not my husband, that's my son," was June's pleased retort. She knew she looked youthful, and she had always promoted it. June also started to enjoy cruises, totaling some thirty or forty over the years, all of them free. She had a friend who was a probation officer but also a travel agent in her free time, and she would have last-minute opportunities to take trips. The one stipulation would be that she use two rooms, and knowing that June was both flexible and free, she would invite her. June always said, "yes."

Carl III said, "I can describe my mom in one sentence. For her sixtieth birthday, she bought herself a 1979 powder blue Corvette."

Chapter 8

Changing Times

Merriam-Webster defines evolution as "a process of change in a certain direction."[63] That forward movement continued to mark the growth of Hammond's Candies when it faced its most momentous transformation in 1997 with its purchase by the West Indies Candy Company. New owners Bob List and Linda Fasano were attracted to Hammond's reputation as the manufacturer of some of the finest hard candies in the country; Ralph Nafziger, who also came on board at that time, says that his association with the Rocky Mountain Chocolate Company, coupled with his accounting background, made him a natural fit for the new venture. He says that he entered the "tasty world of confectionary products in about 1990 and hasn't looked back."[64]

There was a certain irony that the candy canes, lollies and cut rock products that had propelled Carl Sr.'s development of his family business now served as a magnet for outside investors. Emery Dorsey's reputation as a master candy maker added to the enticement. "Without Emery, we wouldn't have bought the company," said List. "He is the expert, and this type of candy-making is certainly a skill."[65]

As the new owners took over management, one of the most noticeable changes was the increase of the payroll, as the number of employees increased from four full-time people and one part-time person to sixty employees by 2002. Sales doubled, tripled and almost quadrupled, swelling from $300,000 in 1997 and crossing the $1 million mark in 1998. However, most visible, especially to drivers traveling along Denver's Colorado Boulevard, was the

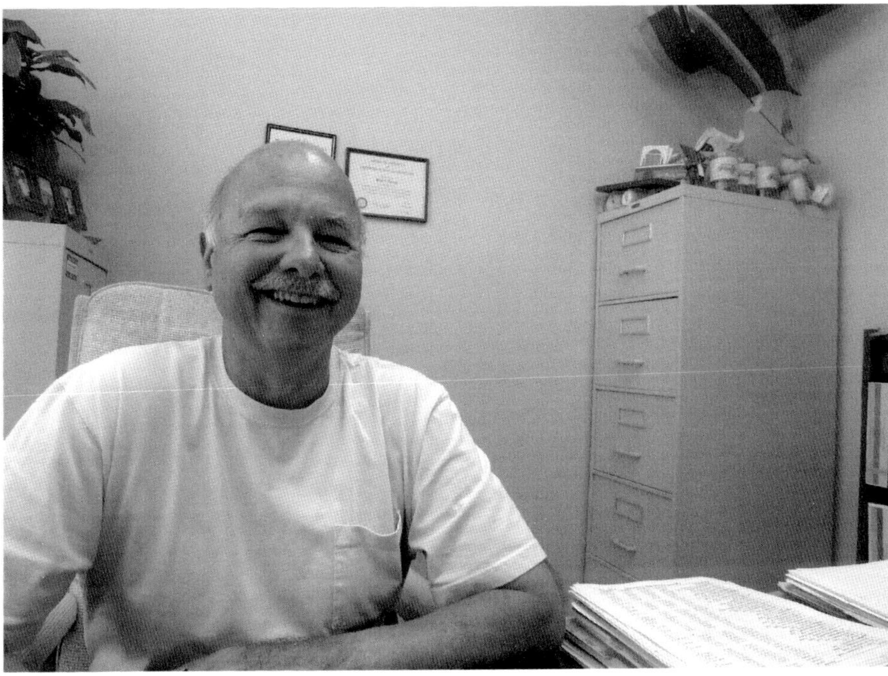

Vice-president of finance and administration Ralph Nafziger, one of the original purchasers of the company from the Hammond family. *Photo by Michael Scalisi.*

new sign atop a bright pink building decorated with a gigantic candy cane and three multicolored lollipops. Hammond's, long a feature of North Denver, had outgrown its second home and moved to a more centrally located spot.

Nafziger, who still serves Hammond's today as vice-president of finance and administration, reiterates that, although the new management made many changes in the business practices, they knew better than to tinker with the methods and recipes that were the foundation of the firm's success. Another kudo underscoring this credo came from a spokesperson from Williams-Sonoma, which had been featuring Hammond's confections for many years: "All the candy from Hammond's is exquisite and delicious. It's almost like little works of art."[66]

In fact, Nafziger says that Williams-Sonoma's business was so important that it practically paid the overhead. For several years, Hammond's sold its English toffee to the chain, adding such goodies as dark chocolate with pecans, milk chocolate with almonds and white chocolate with macadamia nuts. The store sold the toffees in one-pound tins, with one-third of each

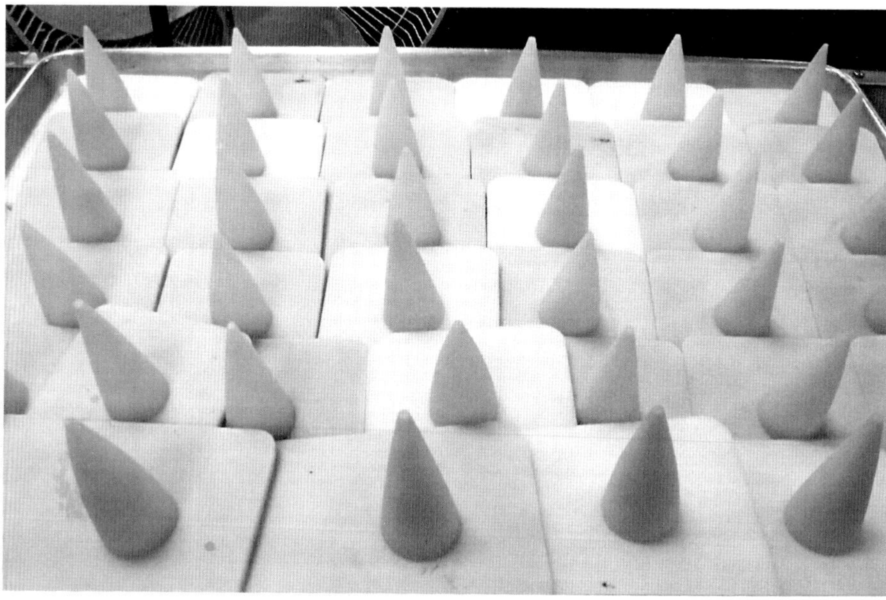

A tray of cones that will be used in forming candy cane trees. *Photo by the author.*

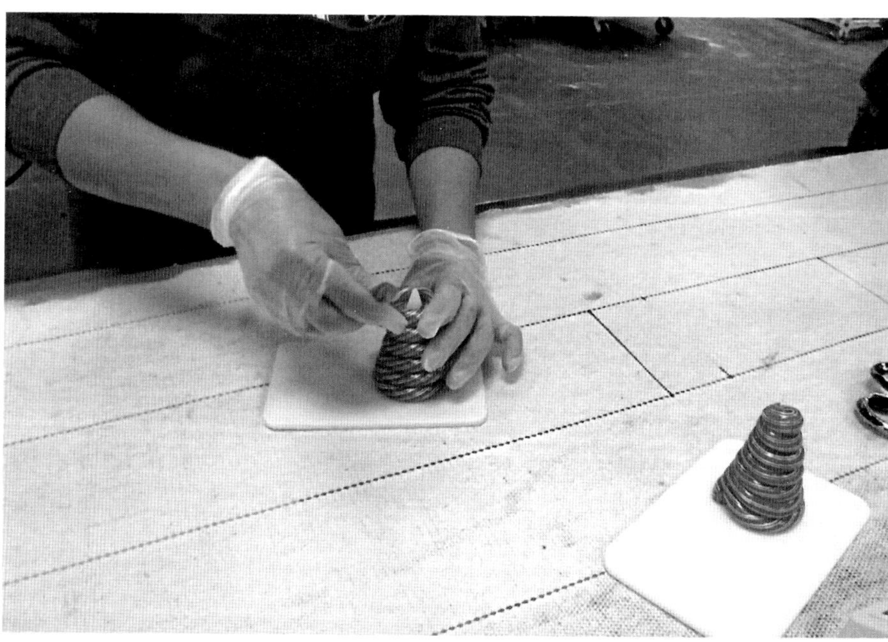

An assistant deftly wraps the pliant rope to form the candy cane trees. *Photo by the author.*

flavor sold per package. Hammond's maintained the same proportion in its sales, since toffee accounted for one million when total sales hit three million.

Other nationally known vendors and giants of the gourmet food industry were highlighting Hammond's confections, including Dean and DeLuca, Vermont Country Store and Martha Stewart, who began to decorate her gingerbread houses with the art candies.[67] Hammond's also enhanced its reputation by becoming known for its ability to exceed special requests. But it is important to note that, despite the overhaul of business practices, small shops throughout the nation continued to repeat their orders year after year. Other changes that gradually occurred involved more sophisticated computerization of files and databases—certainly more efficient but much less colorful than the ledgers of Carl Hammond's early days, when the entries, as well as the confections, were created by hand. In 1999, the *Denver Business Journal* heralded the company as "Denver's Candy Kings."[68]

Another commitment the trio made to further ensure growth was to move toward year-round Christmas candy production. To this end, Hammond's made a long-term capital investment in a humidity-controlled storage space, thus making it possible to produce candies in February and sell them, still fresh, during the holiday season. With the publicity that the website engendered, this also became a practical necessity.

One of the greatest contributions that List, Fasano and Nafziger made to Hammond's Candies was their realization that a recognizable website had become key to business. The world had grown far beyond Yellow Pages and telephone directories, and the desire for instantaneous information gripped consumers. In order to stay current with its competition, Hammond's needed to upgrade its technological appeal. During the 2000 holiday season, Hammond's inaugurated television segments on the Food Network, and the resulting increase in orders swamped the sales force and bogged down phone and fax lines. Hammond's had truly entered the twenty-first century.[69]

In 2004, Hammond's moved from the factory on Colorado Boulevard to its current thirty-five-thousand-square-foot facility at 5725 North Washington Street. Just a few blocks north of I-70 and east of I-25, the new location has made the company more accessible for employees, salespeople and visitors to the popular tours.

Chapter 9

A New Century—A New Look

Hammond's Gets a Facelift

By 2007, Hammond's Candies had become a little bit like everyone's favorite dowager aunt. It had retained the wisdom of age with its treasury of iconic recipes and vintage machinery. Its investment in new products and marketing strategies had increased its sales, but like the money the aunt kept in her voluminous handbag, it wasn't producing profits. Like her annual visit for the holidays, its confections had become an important part of festivals but not something most people thought about buying the rest of the year. Sadly, Hammond's had become a bit fuddy-duddy.

How to adapt the dowager to twenty-first-century living, while at the same time maintaining the legacy of Carl Hammond's small business persona, became a thorny question. The company needed a leader with the same entrepreneurial spirit that had marked the founder's ability to accept new challenges and the flexibility to marry old concepts to modern-day thinking. Enter Andrew Schuman.

For some time, Andy had been exploring the possibilities of a new career as new technologies began to change the way people took pictures and to affect his family's photo business. The rolls of film people had carried in camera bags were quickly being replaced by digital devices, and the local photo shops were giving way to services provided by large chain stores or

Internet companies. A generation was growing up who had never even heard of Kodak.

Fortuitously, Andy, an avid reader of the *Wall Street Journal*, saw the notice that Hammond's Candies was up for sale. The opportunity presented just the challenge he was seeking—a small business that he could buy, make the needed changes and produce the profit that would ensure its future. Hammond's fit that profile and offered one extra attraction: "I liked the confection business," says Schuman.

Andy—who at the time was living in Maryland with his wife, Lori, and three children, Eliza, Joey and Abby—hopped a plane to Denver International Airport and spent two weeks at the facility on Colorado Boulevard. What he found seemed right up his alley. Hammond's had lost the family camaraderie that had characterized its early years under Carl and Tom, and the cultural climate had changed. Andy set out to change all that, to retain the small business feel while introducing a big business plan. He gave himself a year to accomplish his aims—it took him two and a half. It was a great plus for him that Ralph Nafziger agreed to stay under the new ownership.

A conversation with Andy illuminates his perception of his products as additions to America's attraction to cult-like experiences. He cites the examples of people who will go out of their way to buy just a certain kind of coffee, or perhaps have to be home on Tuesday nights to follow the exploits of a particular TV character, or buy only a certain brand of athletic equipment. That experience evokes certain memories and, in a special way, enhances their lifestyle. He wants people to enjoy Hammond's Candies not just because it makes them remember their first Christmas stocking but because it's a yearlong treat that makes their lives feel better and more enjoyable. More S'mores, Peanut Butter and Jelly Sandwich and Candy Cane Crunch are just a few of the candy bar flavors that aren't just good to taste—they make the whole day better!

Open Door

Andy has an open management style; he knows his people and listens to them. People are no longer hesitant to offer their opinions at meetings or stop by his open door, whether it's to discuss a new product idea or something as simple as the wording on a new packaging tag. His employees, all of whom he calls by name, realize that he will give their proposals quick but thorough

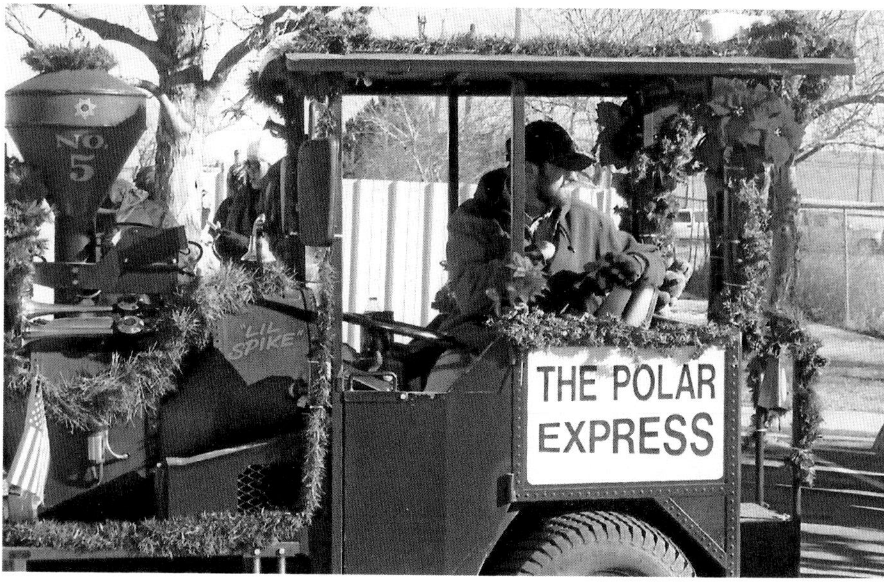

The Candy Cane Festival Polar Express ride delights thousands of visitors each year. *Photo by the author.*

consideration. Always casually dressed—as are all the people in the little cubicles that crowd the office—he is as available to those who work for him, as were the two Carls when they worked side by side making candy canes. In an open-necked shirt or sweatshirt and khakis, he could be considered a modern-day, benevolent dictator because, in the end, he has the final say. However, his staff also knows that he is quick to recognize their potential for growth and promotion; he had been running Hammond's for only a short time when one of the women in packaging became a company rep.

Kammy Stucker's story is another that illustrates that Andy not only oversees what goes on in his company but also sees an employee's potential and offers that person opportunity. Originally an assistant store manager, Kammy had gone to school for pastry and studied fine arts, and she considers the products at Hammond's an art form. She became Hammond's first female candy maker, starting with wedding mints and graduating from soft candies to hard. At first, Kammy says she felt like the Rosa Parks of the kitchen—the men's reactions were a combination of helpful and condescending—but the other women were proud.

Kammy's résumé also includes her stints in public relations, managing the website and retail and mail ordering. She organized and ran the Candy

Cane Festival, Hammond's most popular annual event, which brings ten thousand people to the site every year. Today, Kammy is the company's production manager. Her time as a candy maker gave her the experience to understand that, as she put it, "making candy is a physical operation. Everything is sweating, even your eyelids; your socks are soaking wet; every day you bring the flavors home, and even your toddler notices that you made cinnamon that day." Recognizing Kammy's kind of promise is one of Andy Schuman's hallmarks.

Going Nuts

To increase his company's visibility and recognition factor, Andy directed his energies to rebranding so that there would be a consistent look to all the products. That also included an overhaul of all its marketing materials and catalogues to give them a sharp new appearance that would increase their appeal and sales. A comparison of the sales catalogue used in 2007 with the 2014–15 wholesale brochure underscores the changes that have occurred. When Andy bought Hammond's, materials could have been mistaken for almost any other confectionery business except for the company name. Today, the pages are filled with brightly colored images of every candy available and are presented offering every available type of packaging and product variety. Myriad new products enhance the offerings to wholesalers.

The cover of the current catalogue features a delectable stack of peanut brittle with the promise that "It's official. We've Gone Nuts." Although Hammond's has produced a variety of brittles almost since its inception, its acquisition of the Old Dominion Peanut Company in 2012 has expanded its operations and more than doubled the size of the company, as the combined companies employ close to three hundred people. Their sales outlets run the gamut from the dollar stores to the highest end retailers in the country, and Hammond's candy displays can be found in forty out of the top fifty grocery chains in the country.

In 2010, Hammond's purchase of McCraw's Taffy opened another popular market and added an asset with a history similar to its own. McCraw's Flat Taffy started in a small Texas kitchen with fifty cents' worth of sugar when Dee and Sarah McCraw created their famous and timeless taffy. The taffy recipe has remained unchanged since 1908 and is just as popular today as it was one hundred years ago. The candy comes in a box with approximately twenty-two to twenty-six pieces in assorted flavors. Like Hammond's Honey Ko Kos and Mitchell Sweets, the enjoyment of McCraw's Taffy evokes fond memories of childhood and crosses generational gaps. These are candies that great-grandparents remember and can share with their descendants.

Hammond's Candies has expanded its line of award-winning gourmet chocolate bars with new flavors that range from rich and classic to fun and quirky. Double Chocolate Truffle, Red Velvet Cake, The Cookie Jar, Caramel Mocha and the uniquely sweet and salty Pigs N' Taters have joined such flavors as Peanut Butter and Jelly Sandwich Milk Chocolate Bar, which was named Most Innovative New Product of the Year in 2012 by the National Confectioners' Association. Hammond's repeated this honor in 2013 with the Red Velvet Cake. Hammond's has even turned whoopee pies and cookie dough into candy bars.

The Bee Pollen Chocolate Bar combines the healthy benefits of bee pollen with the rich, satisfying taste of Hammond's organic dark chocolate to create a bittersweet, handmade snack so good that it will make you wonder what took so long for somebody to think of it. Following the tradition set in Hammond's early history when the company worked with schools and nonprofit agencies in their fundraising efforts, 5 percent of profits from new Bee Pollen Chocolate Bars will be donated to bee sustainability efforts. As would be expected, the company is inundated with requests for donations, and candy flies out the door in response.

Hot beverage aficionados also enjoy sweetening their hot cocoa or coffee drinks with the hot cinnamon flavored sugar sticks. These cocoa stirrers are porous, so one can sip while they dissolve and sweeten and flavor the beverage! Other sippers that are available come in lemon, orange, vanilla and peppermint. In 2011, Hammond's entered the gourmet food arena with the launch of its succulent dessert dips and snack pretzels.

Candies are now certified kosher, and the factory receives an annual visit from a rabbi who represents Scroll K/Vaad Hakashrus of Denver. The Scroll K is a nonprofit agency recognized by rabbinical associations, and the Scroll K emblem on a product assures the customer that it is produced with the highest standards of kashrus. All employees must also adhere to strict guidelines for cleanliness and their attire.

Adding to all these developments under Andy Schuman's management, the thread of a family connection has once more been interwoven into the history of this venerable, but thoroughly modern, company. Emery Dorsey, master candy maker and grandson-in-law of Carl T. Hammond, the founder, has returned after a hiatus of several years to assist with product development. There is no doubt that with its dynamic twenty-first-century leadership, Hammond's Candies will continue to delight and enhance the palates of candy lovers for generations to come.

Hammond's Good Manufacturing Practices (GMP)

All personnel engaged in any food handling, preparation or processing operations shall ensure that products and materials are handled and stored in such a way as to prevent damage or product contamination. The methods for maintaining cleanliness include, but are not limited to:

NO—jewelry including: earrings, watches, necklaces, lanyards, body piercings, or rings with stones, etc. Exception: plain band rings, and medical alert necklaces (tucked under clothes).

NO—artificial finger nails or nail polish. Fingernails must be trimmed, filed and maintained so the edges and surfaces are cleanable and not rough.

NO—tobacco usage in the building (smoking in authorized areas ONLY).

NO—gum chewing.

NO—food or drink except in authorized break areas or other approved areas. No open food in lockers.

NO—shorts. Long pants only, in good condition (no holes).

NO—storage of personal items in production area.

NO—carrying pens, pencils, tools, etc. in shirt or coat pockets above the waistline. No pens or pencils behind the ears.

Personal items—coats or sweaters, medicines must be stored in locker or locker area.

Hairnets are to be worn in the kitchen, and packaging areas.
All hair must be contained under the hairnet at all times.
Must be replaced if worn outside, in the break room, or in the restrooms.

Beard Covering must be worn in kitchen and packaging areas,
Must be replaced if worn outside, in the break room or restrooms.

Shirts/Blouses short sleeve or longer (no sleeveless, "spaghetti straps" or tank tops).

- No offensive words or gestures on the shirt.
- No buttons or other sources of physical contamination.
- No glitter or rhinestones or anything that may come loose.

Shoes—must be worn at all times in all areas of the building.

Aprons—must be worn while handling candy in kitchen and/or packaging areas.

- Cannot be worn outside, in restrooms or in break room (within the red lines).
- Must be deposited in marked "dirty apron" locker in break area.
- Must be replaced if dropped on the floor.

Kitchen Personnel—Skull caps or sweat bands must be worn when there is excessive perspiration. Long sleeves or arm covers must be used when carrying batches.

Health Requirements—Any person who appears to have an illness, open lesion, sore, infected wound or any other possible contamination will be immediately assessed and sent home, if necessary, and will not be allowed back into the production areas until a written note from a medical professional releases them. Report such situations to your supervisor immediately.

All these changes have led Hammond's to its current peak performance. In 2014, sales are expected to reach fifteen million.

Candy Tours and Parties

Visitors to the Denver area, as well as those with children from age two on up, will attest that candy factory tours are fun and educational for candy lovers of all ages. Hundreds of thousands of people from across the globe have seen how Hammond's famous, handcrafted candy canes, ribbon candy and lollipops are pulled, twisted and shaped by hand—just like they were in 1920. The Mile High City is home to Hammond's one and only factory location, where guests can see how the candy is handmade and hand packaged from beginning to end. It's a super sweet treat you won't find elsewhere.

The factory tours offer a bit of Colorado-proud history, some tidbits about nostalgic candy, a little science and a lot of fun. With large video screens installed throughout the factory and the tour, everyone gets an up-close-and-personal experience with the delicious candies and the people who make them. This is one opportunity that is sweeter than pie. Making plans to take a tour is easy because no plan is really necessary. No reservations are required for small groups for the tours, which run every half hour (typically on the half hour), Monday through Friday, from 9:00 a.m. to 3:00 p.m., and Saturdays from 10:00 a.m. to 3:00 p.m. The factory is closed on Sundays.

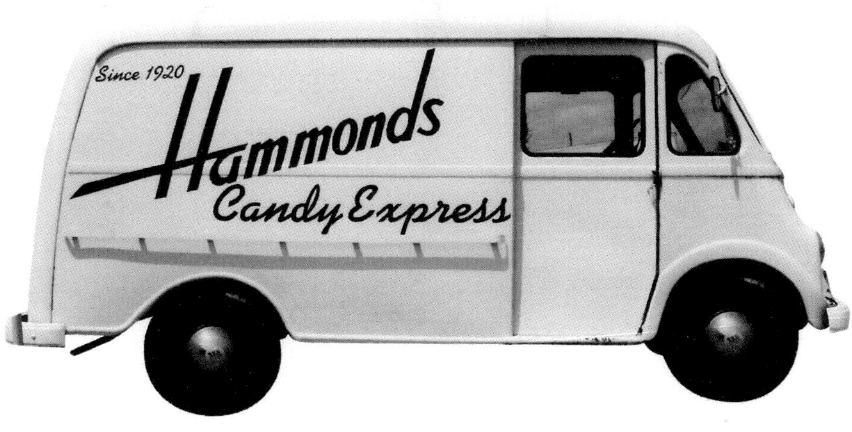

The Hammond's van greets visitors to the candy factory tours. *McBoat Photography, Centennial, Colorado.*

Guests usually receive their first welcome at the front desk from Ginny, who invites them to sign the visitors' book and introduces a short video before the tours, which last approximately thirty minutes, perfect for youngsters. Each tour can accommodate up to fifty people. For little ones with shorter attention spans, the murals on the walls that depict images of the first factory and their employees (look—the men are wearing ties in the kitchen!) are entertaining and offer a view of the past. Everyone is offered one of the hats the workers are wearing, and of course, the tour ends in the gift shop, where every imaginable Hammond's candy is available and shoppers can return home wearing caps, T-shirts, hoodies and even onesies for infants, all adorned with the Hammond logo. Mugs are also available for purchase and are a perfect accompaniment for those trying the sippers and straws. If their children are shopping elsewhere in the store, wary parents can buy bags of coal—just in case. Visitors who arrive early can observe up close a 1960s-era vertical batch roller that was once used to produce Jolly Ranchers hard candies, or they can admire the caramel cooker that the founder, Carl Hammond Sr., used in his first factory in North Denver as far back as the 1930s. Strollers, wheelchairs and walkers are welcome.

"We'd like to make Hammond's a Denver destination," remarked one of the owners before Andy Schuman bought the company. "We'd love for this to become a fun factory experience where people will bring their family or

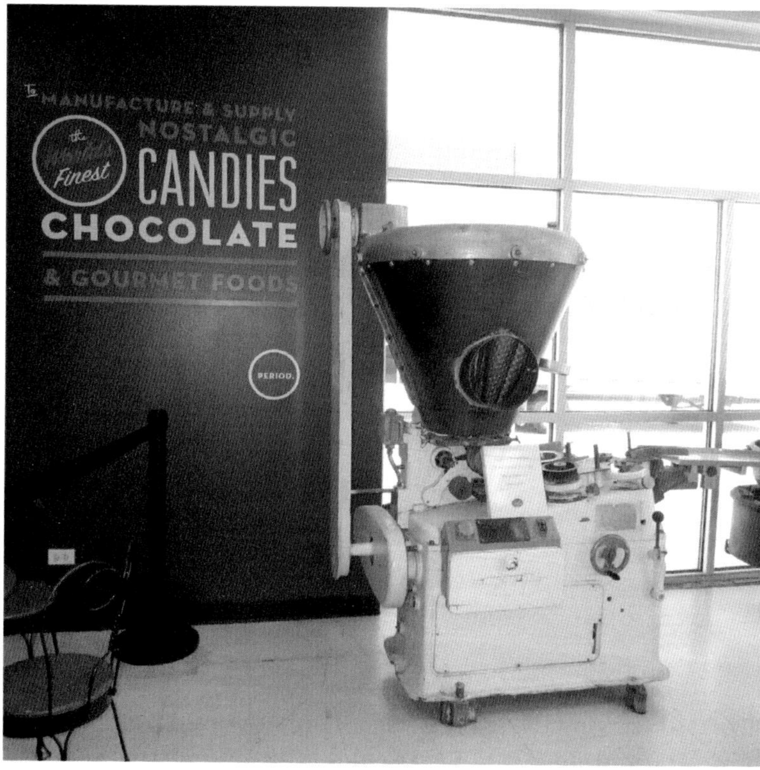

The vertical batch roller from the 1960s on display in the tour office. *Photo by the author.*

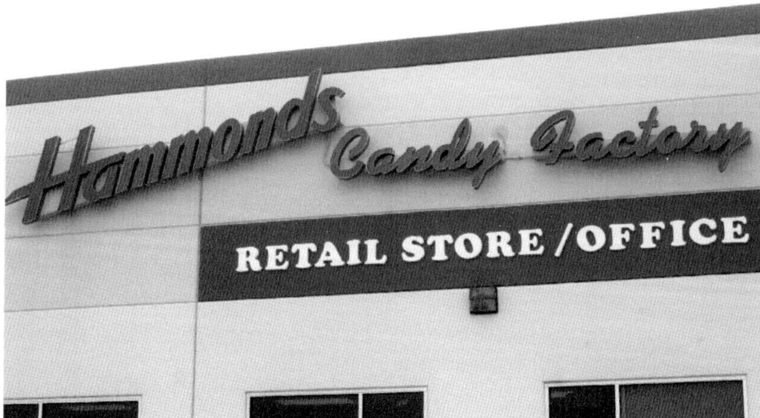

The entrance to the Hammond's Candy Factory on Washington Street in Denver. *Photo by the author.*

guests from out of town. There are people who know where we are already," said Linda Fasano. "We have third-generation customers, and we have customers who come into the store with canes and walkers who wouldn't have Christmas without our ribbon candy."

A visit to Washington Street almost any day at any time of the year shows that people—whether led by guidebooks, word of mouth or a desire to share the memory of a Mitchell Sweet with the next generation—are indeed coming.

Once one has had a "taste" of Hammond's Candy Factory by way of a tour, the next source of delight is a birthday party. It's every child's dream—having their next birthday party in a candy factory! For an amazing, educational and unique experience for a child's birthday party, Hammond's Candies is the sweetest place in town. There are packages that will accommodate every party need. A party at Hammond's will leave children and their friends with memories to treasure for years to come.

Ultimate Candy Experience Birthday Party Package

This package provides an exclusive party in Hammond's 15,000 square-foot candy factory! Guests will be surrounded by thousands of pounds of packaged candy and will be in the middle of Hammond's candy operations as they celebrate that special day!

- *A fully decorated birthday party area in the Hammond's candy factory for two hours*
- *Exclusive candy making experience for each guest*
- *A private, interactive group tour of the candy factory guided by your Hammond's Party Host or Hostess*
- *A Pizza lunch including three large pizzas (cheese or pepperoni); three 2-liter bottles of soda (Coke, root beer, Sprite and lemonade); vanilla and chocolate ice cream cups for every guest. Additional pizzas, sodas and dessert available with additional add-ons.*
- *Gift bags for each guest filled with themed activity books and Hammond's candy.*
- *A large lollipop for the guest of honor.*
- *Hammond's T-shirt for the Guest of Honor.*
- *10% off entire Hammond's Factory Store purchases.*
- *Free Candy of the Day*
- *$595.00 (Up to 24 guests, including Guest of Honor)*

Mitchell Sweets Birthday Party Package

This birthday party package provides use of the Hammond's Birthday Party Room and an up-close look at the Hammond's candy factory for a celebration bursting with sweet flavor!

- *A private, fully decorated birthday party room for two hours*
- *Exclusive candy-making experience for each guest*
- *A private, interactive group tour of the candy factory guided by your Hammond's Party Host or Hostess*
- *A Pizza lunch including: Two large pizzas (cheese or pepperoni); Two 2-liter bottles of soda (Coke, root beer, Sprite and lemonade); vanilla and chocolate ice cream cups for every guest. Additional pizzas, sodas, and dessert available with additional add-ons.*
- *Gift bags for each guest filled with themed activity books and Hammond's candy*
- *A large lollipop for the Guest of Honor*
- *10% off entire Hammond's Factory Store purchases*
- *Free Candy of the Day*
- *$395.00 (Up to 16 guests, including Guest of Honor)*

Chapter 10

Cut Rock Candy Land— A Personal Tour

When the idea was suggested that I might write the story of Hammond's Candies, my very first response was to think, "What fun! Of course, I'll do it." I had fond memories of following my two young grandsons and their nanny on a factory tour not too long after the company started them at its location on Washington Street. But now I had the opportunity to embark on a personal tour. This time, I would be on the side of the glass looking out, not looking in, and I would be reminded that the sense of smell is a seductress.

Before I started, however, I met several people who are key to the backstage performance, because that is what it is. The candy making that I was about to witness is a well-practiced and choreographed routine in which each person's role, like the lines of a play, depends on the previous step being carried out correctly. The candy makers and their helpers truly work in concert.

I was first introduced to Mickey, a diminutive woman who has been with the company since 1982 and came from Laos by way of Des Moines, Iowa. Employees come from countries all over the world, with many related to other employees, and like their predecessors of Hammond's first ninety years, they tend to stay a long time. As someone once noted when these statistics were mentioned, it's a "sweet" place to work. Mickey has been a candy packer, a chocolate dipper and is now the manager of packaging, but while I was there, I also watched her crooking the canes. She worked with both Tom and Emery and remembers when Robin helped in the office.

When I asked her what has kept her at Hammond's so long, she replied that she loves working with candy and that all her employers have made her feel valued as an employee. That's why visitors can sense the pride Maria and Monica show as they fill the jars with peppermint pillows or why Valentina and Chandra fill each bag of hard mix so carefully. I watched Carmen as she lined up the jars for Liz and Karina straightening the boxes for the next packagers. Gregoria and Saroj were sorting and weighing at the gleaming metal tables, while Liap sealed the canes in their sleeves.

Before chatting with Mickey, I had removed my rings and other jewelry and left them in one of the offices before another woman checked that I was wearing long pants, closed shoes and a shirt with no buttons. Now I was ready for my adventure into candy making—as soon as I settled a hairnet on my head. In the early years, the kitchen workers wore hats similar to the ones that visitors receive when they take the regular tour, but hairnets were introduced and became mandatory in about 1997.

To enter the kitchen proper, I first walked through the packaging department, a mini tour that in itself is an education. Not only are the candies handmade, but most tins and bags are packed by hand, and the ribbons are first formed into bows and then attached with the tags to the packages. That day, the peppermint candy cane trees were being packaged, so the ties were red. The workers talk softly among themselves occasionally, but each detail is carefully checked, and you can see the pride they take in their work. I particularly enjoyed meeting Lillian, Geraldine and Tay as they attached labels to the cellophane sleeves for the candy canes. Collectively, the three of them have worked at Hammond's for forty-one years, and like proud proprietors, they have greeted me warmly on my subsequent visits.

Just behind that trio were the clear vertical blinds that separate the two sections and lead to the main part of the kitchen where the cooking takes place. My first impression was of a fairly large room with overhead lights that reflect on shiny metal tables or, even more inviting, on sheets of candy that glow warmly. A long row of huge copper kettles and fire mixers lined one wall, and interspersed throughout the room were a variety of mysterious-looking machines that I would gradually see in motion. It was here that I met Victor, the kitchen manager and my tour guide for the afternoon. Victor has been at Hammond's for twelve years. He would captivate me completely as he led me from start to finish, from corn syrup to the beautiful cut rock menorahs he was making that day. When he first told me that was what he would be creating, I was at a total loss, since the

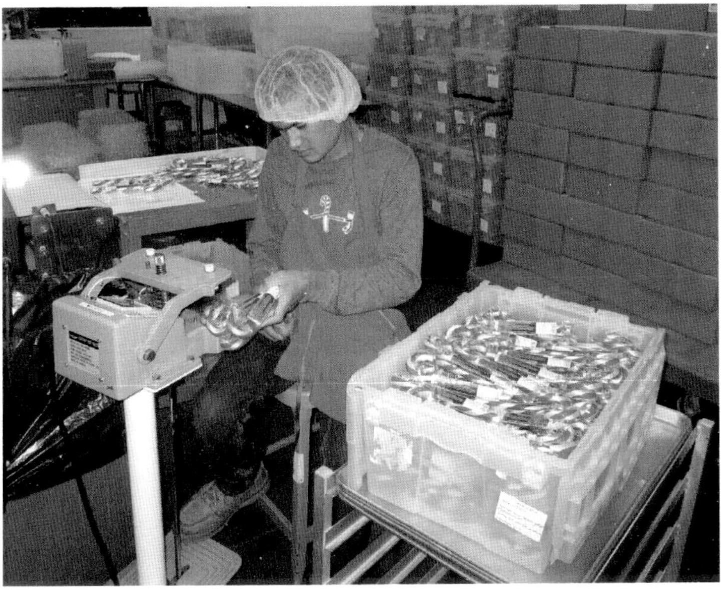

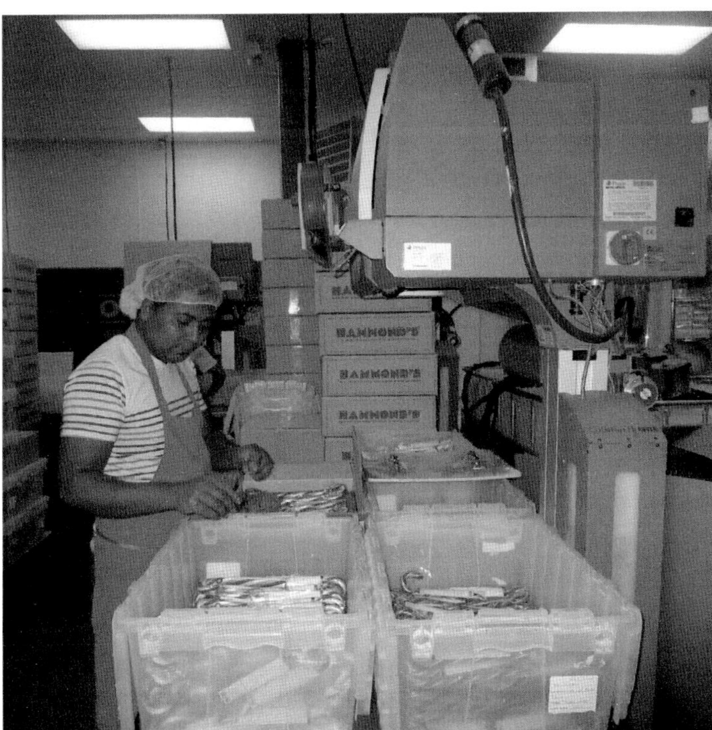

Top: Sealing individual candy canes to protect them from humidity. *Photo by the author.*

Left: A kitchen assistant boxes the ever-popular candy canes in the busy packaging room. *Photo by the author.*

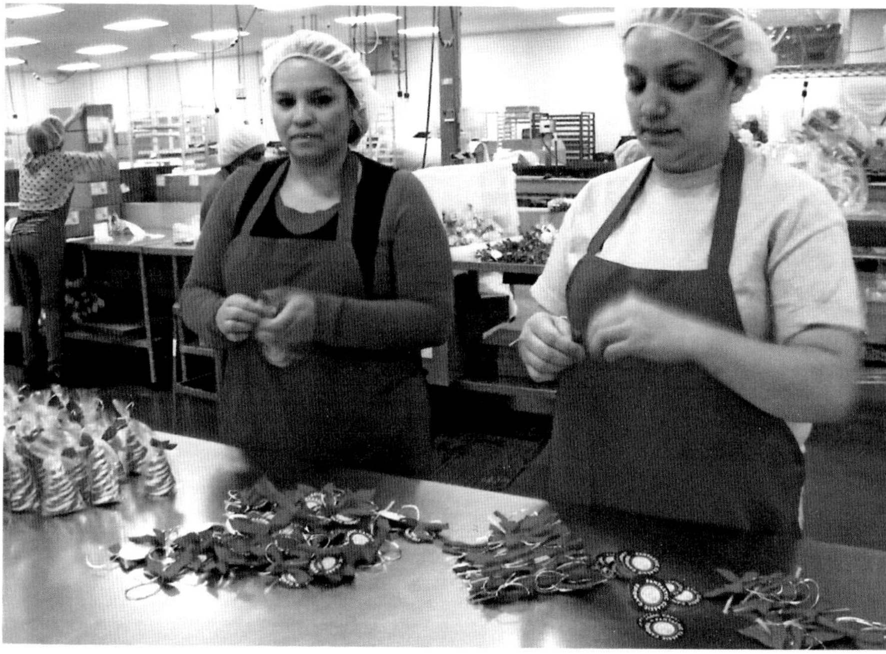

Hand-tying red ribbons and tags to each packaged candy cane tree. *Photo by the author.*

only menorahs I could imagine were similar to candelabra, and I doubted that was correct.

Before Victor and I started, I learned that it takes from six months to two years to learn to be a cook, and one has to be big like Jesus, who was busy moving candy from one table to the next, or Gustavo, who was folding and pressing the flavoring into another slab. A person doesn't have to be big to shape the candy canes, but it's necessary to be quick, I realized, as I saw Amber dividing lengths of peppermint while Boun shaped them into canes. Fernando was cutting more candy into longer strips to be coiled into lollipops. Later, Khem would box them for shipping to wholesalers.

Unquestionably the largest piece of equipment in the kitchen, the corn syrup tank is a gleaming behemoth that holds, Victor explained, thirty thousand pounds. It has a sizeable spigot that dispensed the clear liquid into one of the kettles that he had settled into a wheeled stand. Sometimes, he also used a shiny bucket to add more of the syrup. Next, Victor hefted one of the bags of sugar from a nearby stack to pour into a pot and then added water from a large measuring pitcher, all the while mixing it with a sturdy stirrer made from an axe handle. The proportions for this batch

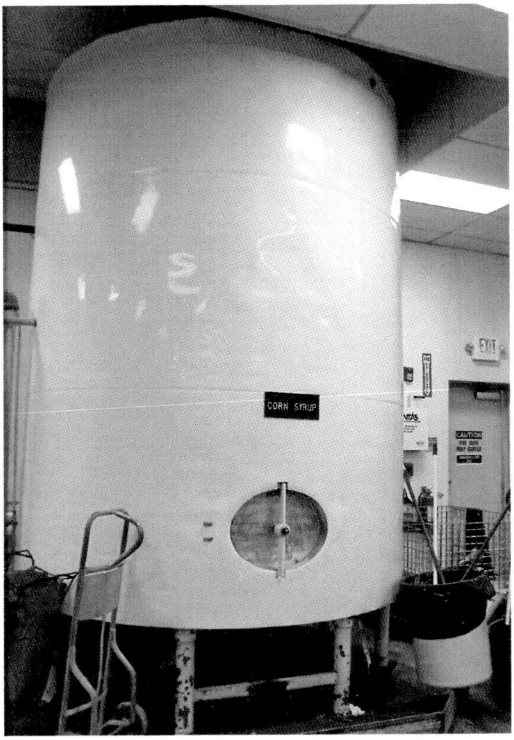

Left: The corn syrup tank holds thirty-five thousand pounds. *Photo by the author.*

Below: Candy maker Victor measuring corn syrup for the "menorah" cut rock candies. *Photo by the author.*

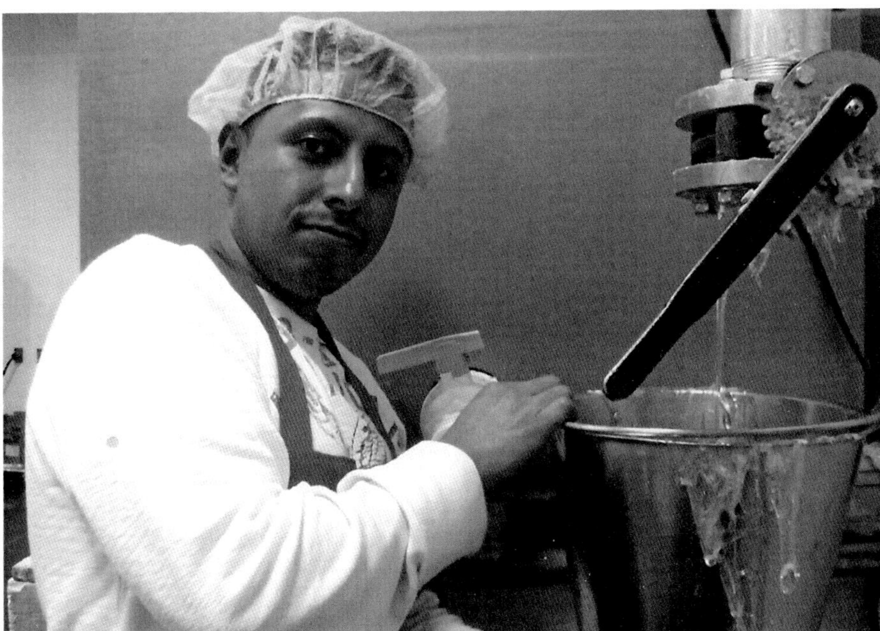

would be forty-four pounds of sugar, thirty-three pounds of corn syrup and five quarts of water, a very heavy mixture that he wouldn't have been able to move without the cart. Wheeling it over to the stoves, he needed Delano's assistance to lift it into the base of the fire mixer. Nearby, Parshu stirred another steaming kettle while Ibrahim worked at yet another table.

Carl Sr. knew just from looking at the bubbling mass when it had reached the critical temperature, but less experienced candy makers always rely on a thermometer. Today's cooks have the benefit of an automatic temperature gauge on the fire mixer. When that exact moment is reached—too low and the syrup won't set, too high and it will burn—heavily gloved hands removed the kettle and then very carefully poured the candy syrup onto the cooling table. Although no one seemed to be in a hurry, they moved with deft precision, since timing is important to maintain the temperature. Once one has tasted any Hammond's Candies—and the purity of the taste makes it unforgettable—it is hard to comprehend that such elementary objects are used as tools. A worker may use a saw blade to run under the candy on the table to keep it from sticking, carpet shears to cut the candy and steel bars beveled at the ends to turn and knead the hard candy. While the candy was still spread on the table, I watched as color and flavoring were added before the fifty-pound slab was moved to the construction table. I was no closer to understanding what Victor had meant when he spoke about a menorah, so I watched with rapt attention as he and Keo, a short, wiry man of indeterminate age, started to manipulate the block. Behind Victor, against the wall, a rather odd contraption with protruding arms stood quietly idle until Victor approached, cradling a large block of candy in his arms. Before I knew what he was doing, he had wrapped his bundle around the arms, and then it was whirling and twisting and getting longer and lighter in color as air was worked into the mass. I suddenly realized that what I was watching was a process similar to what in a much smaller way had happened in my kitchen when my Girl Scouts attempted a taffy pull. This was much prettier to see. The machine is the puller, which lightens the candy's color and adds air to it.

Gradually, Victor and Keo repeated these steps, forming the different layers with alternating dark amber and pale cream sheets of the candy. At one point, Victor looked at me, saying, as he worked on a bright yellow slab, "Now I'm forming the flame." Sure enough, I could see as I studied the large block he was gently rolling back and forth that the end of the block resembled a menorah. But this was my first glimpse of the creation of a cut rock candy, and I still didn't have any idea of what would happen next. I didn't have long to wait. He carried the large chunk over to what he

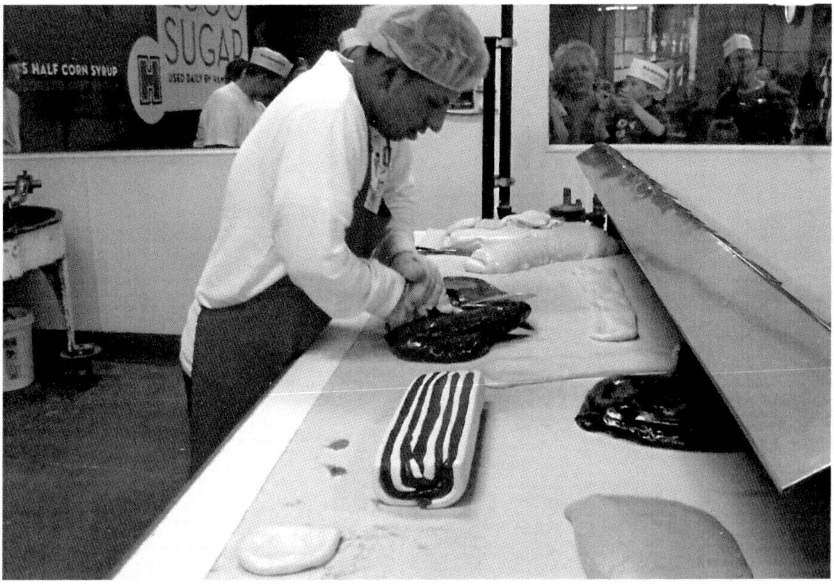

Colored layers of candy are molded into a design at the construction table. *Photo by the author.*

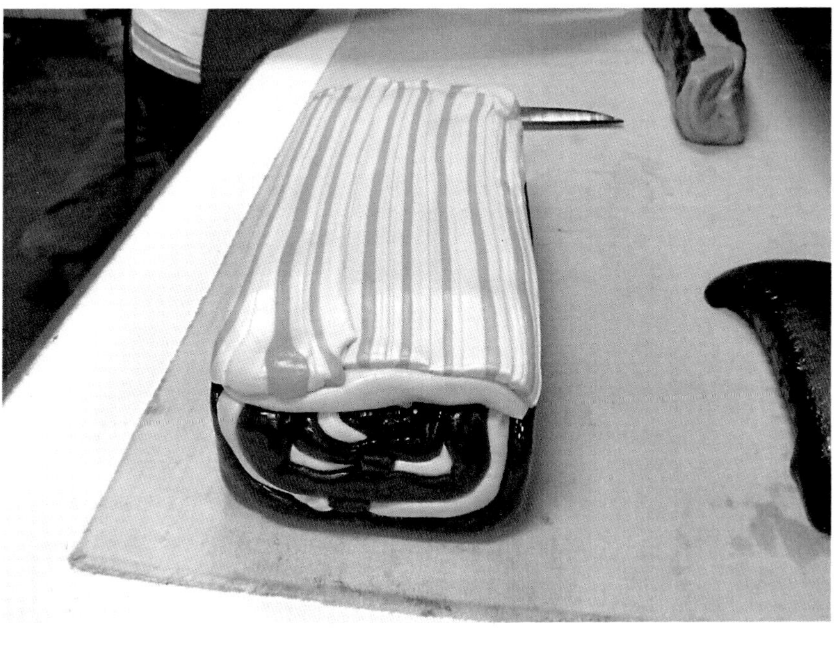

The block of candy showing the menorah design. *Photo by the author.*

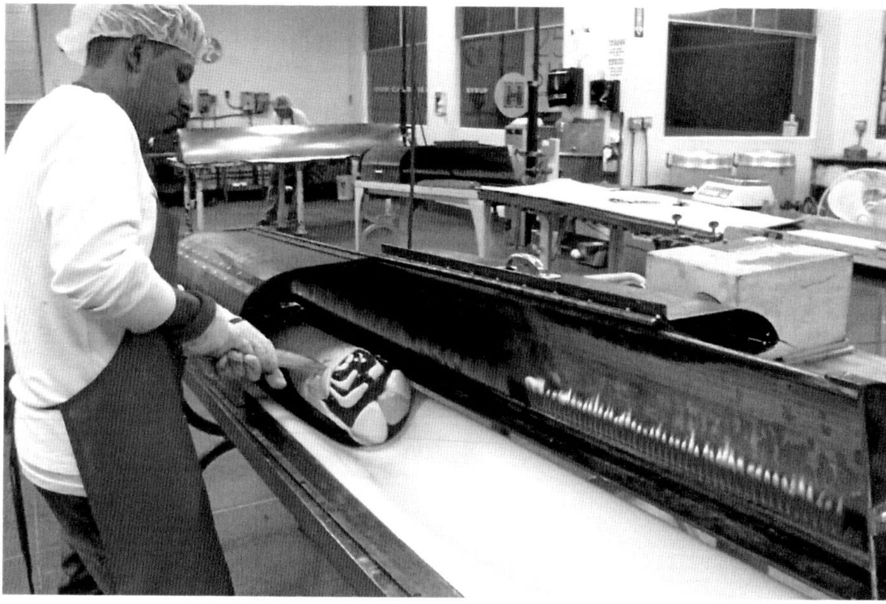

Victor works at the batch roller, where the block is kept warm and pliable and formed into a round shape before being stretched into a slender rope for cutting. *Photo by the author.*

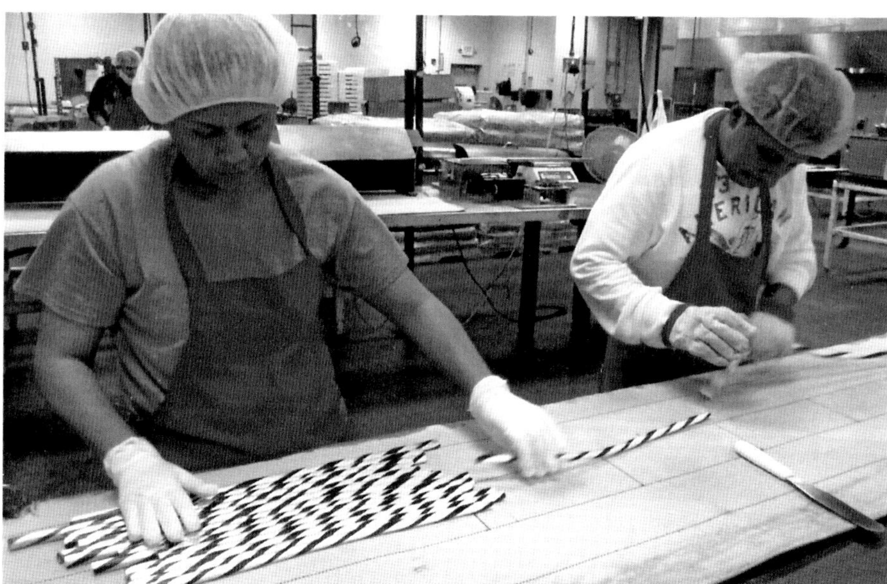

A kitchen assistant quickly cuts the rope that Victor has molded—a process that expert candy makers know by "feel and touch." *Photo by the author.*

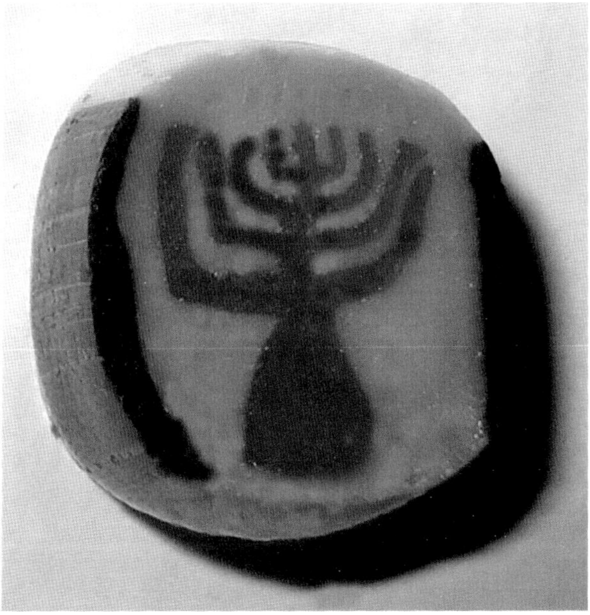

The menorah art candy. *Photo by the author.*

told me was the batch roller, a long canvas cradle that rocked the candy back and forth in front of a bright—and hot—row of gas jets. As I watched the block start to get longer and narrower, Victor suddenly grabbed it, and with movements so quick and deft that his gloved hands became indistinct blurs on my camera, I saw that what had just a moment before been an indistinct menorah was now a long candy about one-half inch in diameter with a perfectly centered little menorah. Seconds later, one of the women fed it into the candy cutter, and I went home that afternoon with a bag of candies to share with my grandsons. I couldn't wait to come back for a lesson in chocolate.

Chapter 11

Dipping into Chocolates—My Second Behind-the-Scenes Tour

I've always thought it is a good thing that there are no calories attached to the aroma of candy, because if there were, a visit to Hammond's on a day that the chocolates are being made would be disastrous to anyone's waistline. Fortunately, the impact is, instead, merely a sensual experience, a delight to the eye and a mouth-watering moment as the bouquet of the chocolate flavors the air. On the day I arrived for my tour, I thought for a second I might need to hide my hands behind my back to keep from plucking a morsel from a passing tray and popping it into my mouth.

Now that the impressions of my first visit had settled, I began to notice other machinery spotted around the factory floor and marveled at the apparent age of much of the equipment. In chatting with Kammy, the production manager, I was reminded that many of the pieces date to the earliest years of the company and had probably been used by Carl Sr. I knew he had almost always purchased his machinery secondhand, and frequently from Savage Bros., which has continuously manufactured confectionery machinery for over 150 years. I felt somewhat awed since this meant that many of the pieces had been in use for well over 100 years. That is an amazing concept in what has been dubbed a throwaway society and shows that the values Carl instilled in his family and employees thrives to this day. One of these pieces of machinery, the melter, had already been put into service earlier before I had arrived for my tour. First, though, I needed to discover a little bit about the chocolate that smelled so good.

Candy makers can choose to purchase chocolate in several forms: in buttons, bars or delivered as a warm liquid for those that can take truckloads.

Hammond's has always purchased ten-pound bars and melted them in one of the melters I had noticed. Over the years, Hammond's has consistently used Ambrosia, Guittard and Merckens chocolate, which comes from beans. Candy makers buy from them to make their own products and flavors. The industry has gotten a lot more sophisticated in the flavor profiles it likes, but the dark chocolate has gotten the most attention for its health qualities.

Once the chocolate is delivered, someone breaks up the bars and loads the melter. Next the chocolate is melted, and dairy buckets are filled with the liquid to replenish the levels in the enrober. The chocolate levels get lower as whatever candy centers are being coated pass under the chocolate wall, or waterfall, as some would call it. The tempering at Hammond's usually takes place in the enrober. This process takes from three to five people, depending on what candy is fed through it.

I had already learned a little bit about the tempering process, which basically entails the proper melting, cooling and distribution of cocoa butter in the chocolate, and I knew from firsthand experience what happens if it isn't done properly. I had tried many times to achieve professional-looking chocolate-covered strawberries in my own kitchen, and I had never been satisfied since they lacked a pleasing, shiny appearance. Even with that small amount of technical knowledge, I wasn't prepared for the sight of the chocolate softly whirring in the tempering wheel. The sight was awesome and beautiful and difficult to describe. The candy makers were preparing to make toffee that day with milk chocolate, which, when in the tempering process, becomes a silky, shimmering mass of liquid beauty.

By this time, the women who were making the chocolates that day were lining up the squares of toffee in the feeding area of the enrober, carefully inspecting each one prior to setting it on its way to the pre-bottomer, where the confection receives its first layer of chocolate. As it travels along on a canvas conveyor belt, it rides over a chocolate-coated grate that is propelled by two tempering wheels; then, once that first chocolate is applied, it moves on a canvas belt that propels it through the enrober, which will coat it entirely. As it reappeared, Fee carefully marked it with its proper string before it proceeded to the temperature-controlled tunnel and the takeoff area.

As I watched these proceedings, I was once again impressed with the dexterity and the unhurried, yet precisely timed, steps that were followed. Some of these candies might be destined for a specialty shop on Fifth Avenue in New York City; others might be featured on the newest television food show; still others might grace an elaborate dinner party, but regardless of

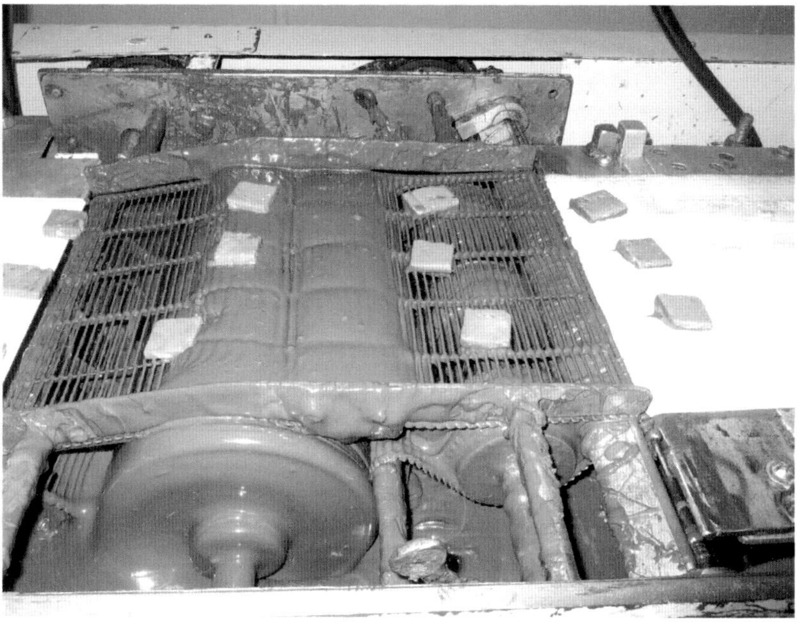

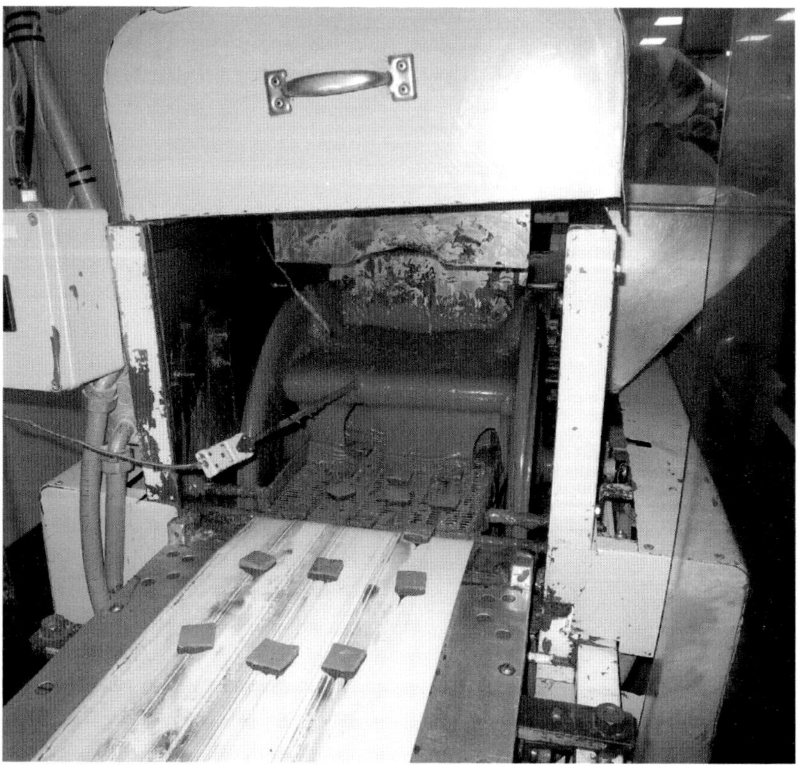

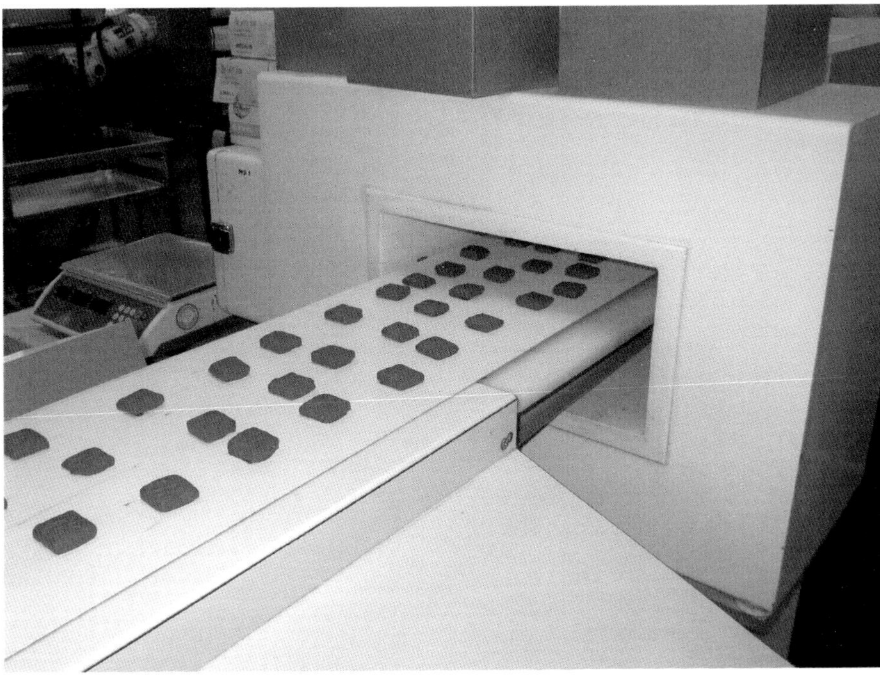

Above: Chocolates emerge from the temperature-controlled tunnel on their way to packaging. *Photo by the author.*

Opposite, top: The pre-bottomer coats toffee with its first layer of chocolate. *Photo by the author.*

Opposite, bottom: The toffee passes through the "waterfall" of chocolate in the enrober. *Photo by the author.*

their destination, all had to fulfill the important requirements for Hammond's quality. At one point, I noticed that all activity had paused, and looking down the line, I realized that one of the assistants had momentarily left her position in the proceedings. Again, as in all well-choreographed performances, each step has to follow in its well-ordered sequence. The production of chocolate candies that will result in a perfectly shaped confection that glows with a pleasing sheen is no exception. With her return, the process started anew, and soon more toffee was emerging from the cooling tunnel. Yasmen stood ready to nestle the chocolates in their paper cups and skillfully arrange them in boxes. Perhaps one of them might become a birthday or anniversary present or a welcome hostess gift.

Just a few steps away from the enrober, Akuwa was teaching Lily the first steps in the art of truffles. The experienced cook was filling tiny molds that had already been drizzled with dark chocolate as a decorative touch to the exterior of the candy. Gently tilting the pan so that the sides of each cup were properly coated, she then poured out the excess chocolate. While those molds settled, she filled the ones she had previously formed with a ganache center. The pan was then placed on a machine that vibrated the candies to remove any bubbles that might have formed. After that, they were ready for the bottoms to be added to seal the entire confection. Yum.

Saying goodbye, I walked past the cutting machine, where Josie was feeding bright orange ropes into the equipment and bright candies were tumbling into the basket below. What an afternoon I had enjoyed—I hadn't gained an ounce, but I had gained a new insight into the art of candy making.

On my way to the exit, I paused to wave to a group of children who were on a tour on the other side of the window and turned to see what they were watching with rapt attention. Two of the assistants at a nearby workstation were deftly turning out jewel-toned ribbon candies, using one of the most intricate pieces of equipment in the factory. As in the creation of cut rocks, the first helper was preparing the candy for the machine, in this case stretching and smoothing it into a perfectly flat ribbon that was just the correct width. The second man was feeding the stream of still pliable candy into the ribbon crimper that is composed of a complex series of cogs and gears. Once the ribbon was crimped, the piece was being pushed together and gently guided down a long, narrow slide and allowed to cool. The gas-fired table heaters must be maintained at 160 degrees to keep the candy pliable. It is then cut to precisely the required length to fit the candy box. Ribbon candy is almost as symbolic of the holidays as its hard candy cousin, the candy cane, and admiring the brilliance of the ribbon candy was like finding a rainbow at the end of my second factory tour.

Appendix A

Excerpts from the Eulogy for Carl Thomas Hammond Jr.

by Carl Thomas Hammond III

We're here today to celebrate the life of my father, Carl Thomas Hammond Jr. He was born in Denver to Carl Thomas Hammond and Laura Johnson Hammond on April 2, 1922. He died on February 2, 1985. To all his friends, he was known as Tom.

He was the president of the Hammond Candy Co. and master candy maker. My dad made twenty different hard candies at Christmas—candy canes, ribbon candy, hard candy filled with nut meats, cut rock—a complete line of chocolates, five different fudges, seven different brittles, ten different caramel items, twenty different Easter eggs, wedding mints and on and on. More than 150 items all made from scratch. Even some of his raw materials were made, such as marshmallows. I know people whose saliva runs at the mention of banana marshmallow eggs dipped in dark chocolate.

He was a craftsman at candy making. He cooked by sight and feel and smell. When I asked one day at what temperature he would test the caramel, he replied, "Oh, you know, when it is kind of a golden brown." Making candy that way with the consistency he did over the years, it becomes almost an art.

I don't know how many master candy makers there are with the skill of my father, but after talking to many people in the business, surely there are not more than a handful who produce and sell the variety that my dad did. And when I realize that there are some 250 million people in the U.S., being one of a handful is very special.

As a businessman, he was well respected. He was honest and sincere. One Christmas, we were discussing the pricing on candy canes. The previous year, they had sold for twenty-five and thirty-five cents wholesale and retail. Our costs had gone up, and I knew that the only other handmade and hand-wrapped candy canes anyone could buy wholesale were seventy-five cents. So he decided thirty-five cents wholesale. I told him that even our customers thought that thirty-five cents was more than reasonable. “No,” he said, “that is more than enough for us.”

What a refreshing response in a capitalistic economy where profit is king. And there is a deeper significance to his statement. It involves being comfortable with who you are and what you are doing and knowing what is really important to you. My dad had that knowledge, and he ran a successful, profitable small business. He never borrowed money, and he never had an unprofitable year. Success is ultimately measured within yourself. My dad was a successful person.

His fondest love, outside his family, I believe was horses. He belonged to the Palomino Mounted Patrol, holding practically every office, including bartender. He thoroughly enjoyed riding. At times, in the summer, he would go out after work and ride. I remember him saying that he could go out and ride for an hour and feel like a new man. In another era, I can see him saddled, working cattle, on what our family affectionately calls Grandpa’s mountain.

His horses, I believe, made him young in spirit. He was always trying to do things better. Several years ago, before computers were the rage, he bought a personal computer for his business, and he asked me to show him how to use it. A youthful attitude can accomplish much at any age.

His most visible virtue was his general outlook on life. He honestly believed that everything happens for the best. So he constantly looked for the best and good in every situation. He didn’t have problems; he had opportunities. Some days he would say, “I could do with a few less opportunities.” He believed that you were as good as you felt, and he felt great. This constant positive attitude carried him successfully through many physical ailments, without complaint, and he rarely missed a day of work.

He was a person who was easy to meet and easy to talk to. He was a good person, a genuine person. A person you respected. And best of all, he wore his virtues quietly.

As a husband, he was loving and compassionate. There was never any doubt as I grew up that my father and mother loved each other very much. They were a constant example to me of how two people could share their lives with purpose and fondness.

One of my brothers, George, also a father, said it very well in a verse he found in a song by Dan Fogelberg:

I thank you for the music,
and your stories of the road.
I thank you for the freedom
when it came my time to go.
I thank you for your kindness
and the times when you got tough.
And Papa, I don't think I said
"I love you" near enough.

And that is the good news. The virtues that he lived so quietly and so well don't pass with him. They are passed on to those who knew him and loved him, especially his family. They were passed on, for example, to me to live the best I can, and I will pass them on to others and my children just as his father had done and his grandfather before him.

I would like to close by sharing a recent memory I have of my father. He was at a gathering talking with some friends. There was laughter in his eyes and a broad smile on his face. As he talked, he laughed spontaneously. That is how I will always remember him—as a very happy man. I hope each of you have happy memories of my dad. He was a happy person in love with life and the people in it.

Appendix B

About Andrew Schuman

Andrew Schuman, president and CEO of Hammond's Candies, graduated from the University of Wisconsin–Madison with a BA in international relations and economics and continued graduate studies, receiving an MBA in finance from the George Washington School of Business and Public Management.

While attending graduate school, Andrew began working in his family's business, operating a chain of franchised photo-processing locations under the trade name Motophoto. He became a principal in the Washington, D.C. metropolitan market as an area sub-franchisor. He was actively involved in management, operations and servicing of new and existing franchise locations. Over the fifteen years Andrew was involved in the family business, he engineered the acquisition and sale of more than twenty different companies as part of the regional growth, managing in excess of $25 million in annual sales. Andrew was awarded the President's Award at the Motophoto International Convention in 2001 for superior performance as a multiple-unit franchisee and for his contributions to the company's franchise system.

In early 2006, after several challenging years in a changing market, he made the tough decision to divest his interest in the family business and actively seek a new venture that would be equally as challenging and rewarding. In the spring of 2007, Andrew completed the acquisition of Hammond's Candies. Since the purchase, he has served as president and CEO while presiding over the board of directors.

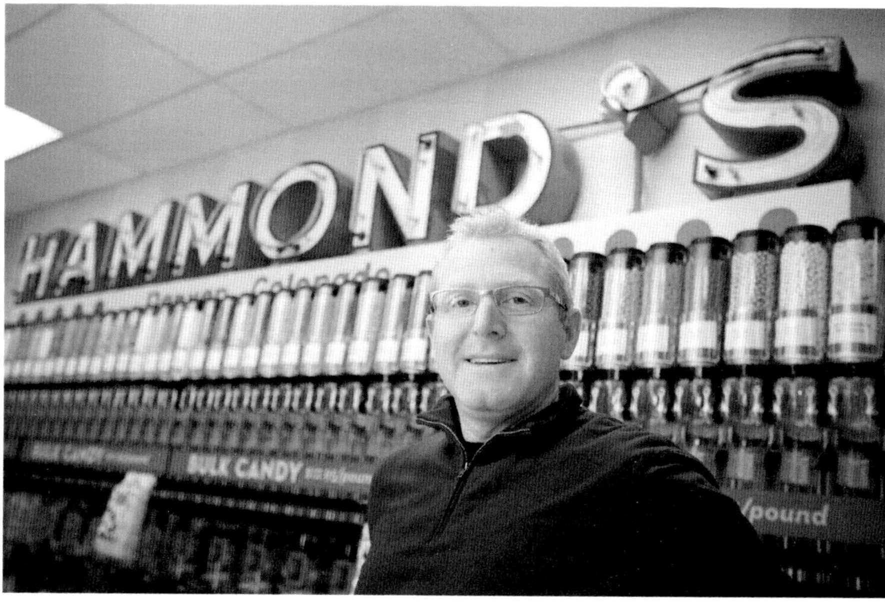

CEO Andrew Schuman in the Hammond's Candy gift shop. *McBoat Photography, Centennial, Colorado.*

During the first five years of Andrew's ownership, Hammond's grew 130 percent to $12 million in revenue. The manufacturing workforce has grown from 60 to 120 permanent associates and seasonally employs up to 150 individuals. In June 2011, under Andrew's leadership, the company was recognized as one of the "50 Colorado Companies to Watch." The company has been recognized with multiple awards for branding, innovative packaging and design.

Appendix C

Glossary of Terms and Processes

BATCH ROLLER: A batch roller has two large poles wrapped with a cotton tarp. The poles turn the cotton tarp, and as the candy is turning, it keeps the pressure the same on all sides, giving the candy its nice round shape. It allows the candy maker to create a candy rope for candy canes, lollipops and other hard candies more efficiently. A gas line runs at the base of the hood, and an open flame keeps the candy hot and pliable. Gas gives a constant heat and doesn't fluctuate up and down.

BEATER CONFECTIONS: These include fondants, fudge and cream centers.

CANDY CANES AND LOLLIPOPS: Candy canes and lollipops are made at Hammond's year round. Each batch starts out at seventy-seven pounds but can become larger depending on the amount of recycled candy added. (Recycled candy comes from previous batches, usually the first or last pull or pieces that don't come out just right. About five to ten pounds of recycled candy is added right after the candy is poured onto the cooling tables, and any existing flavor burns off at this time.)

Candy is usually cooked between 320 and 330 degrees, depending on the type of candy being made. Once it reaches the desired temperature, it is poured onto the cooling tables, which have been rubbed down with coconut oil. Color, flavor and—if it is a fruit flavor—citric acid are added at this time. The candy is divided into what is the center of the candy and the stripes. This is done with one of the cooks' most valuable tools: those big carpet scissors. The cooks continue to turn the candy onto the cooled tables with a large stainless steel pole until it cools to a temperature they can mold

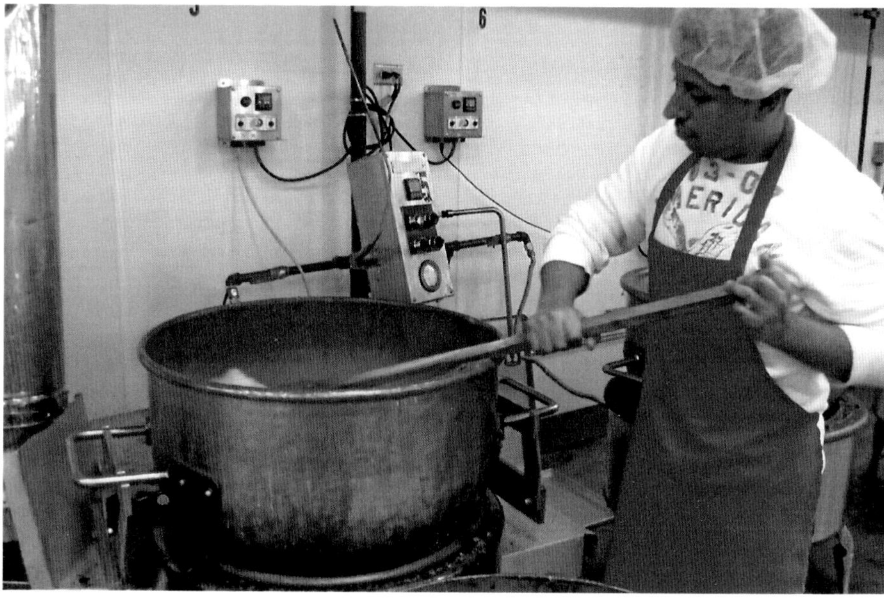

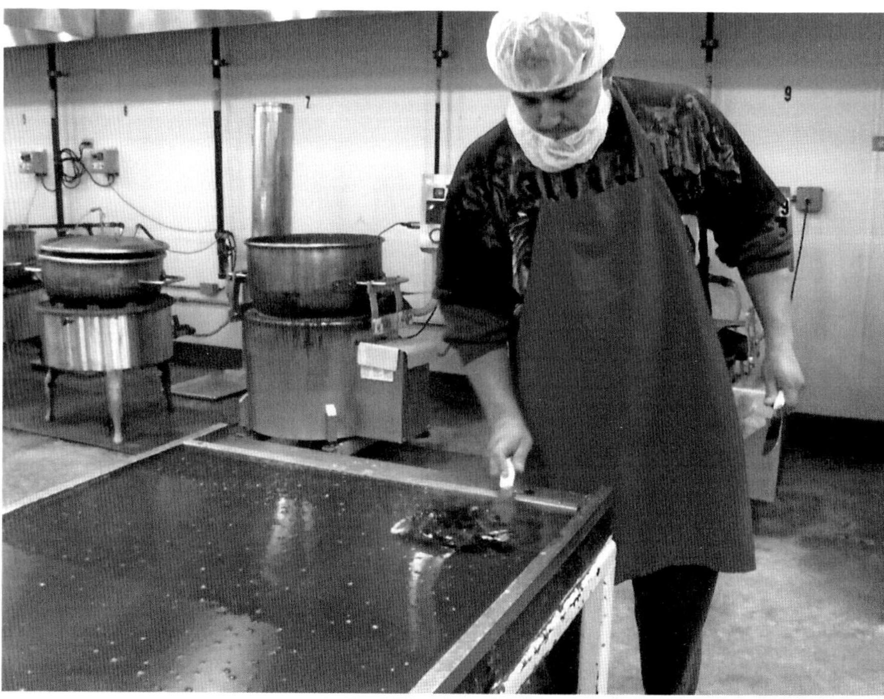

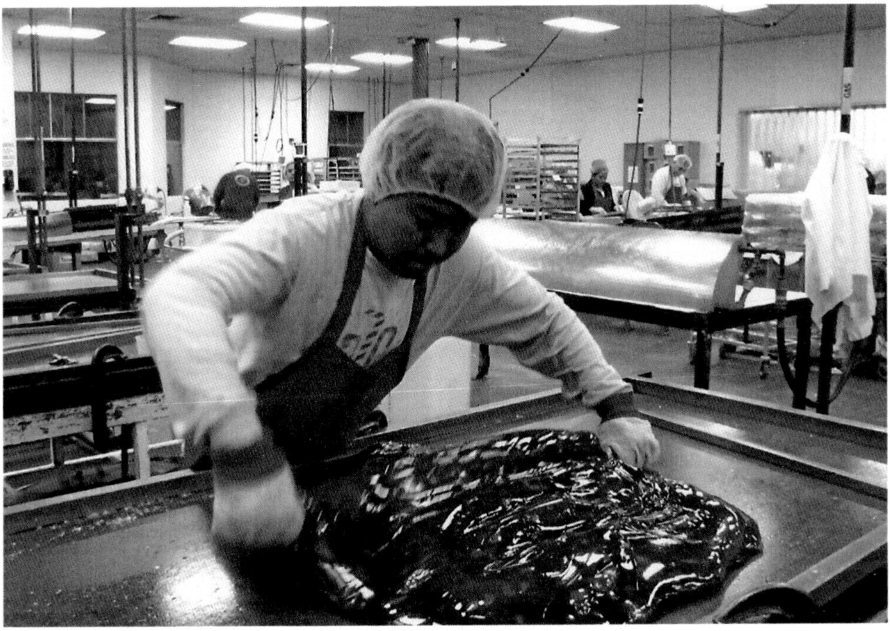

Opposite, top: Cooking the candy to about 325 degrees. *Photo by the author.*

Opposite, bottom: Adding color and flavoring for hard candies. *Photo by the author.*

Above: A cook spreading and flattening the flavored batch on the cooling table. *Photo by the author.*

with their gloved hands. The temperature of the candy is estimated at about 220 degrees at this time. Once the candy is at this point, it is moved to the "blocking table."

Pieces of the candy are put on the candy puller to lighten the color of the candy pieces and then kneaded to remove the lines that were formed from the puller. Once the ideal color is achieved, the cooks will begin the stripe building process. Depending on the pattern, blocks of candy will be stretched into long strips of candy and placed accordingly next to each other, forming the stripe pattern. The center of the candy is also placed on the candy puller, where the flavor is added. Candy cane and lollipop centers are different from each other; the center for the candy canes are mixed only long enough to mix the flavor in, whereas the lollipop centers are on the puller for at least two minutes, making it more light and fluffy, so it is easier to twist. Once the centers have been pulled, they will be formed into a block shape, and larger air bubbles that are formed during the pulling process will be punctured with the scissors and finally wrapped with the jacket. With the filled canes, the center will be spread out onto the table looking like a three-foot by three-foot flat piece of candy. A fresh batch of cream filling (either chocolate or vanilla cream) is prepared (by another cook) and is placed in the center of the candy. The candy is then wrapped around the cream and sealed, shaped into a block and wrapped with the striped jacket. These batches can be as heavy as one hundred pounds. At this point, the cook will hand carry the large piece of candy to a batch roller.

When the candy is ready to pull, the cook will begin to push the candy at the end, making it into a smaller diameter easier to grab with both hands. A small piece of the batch will be pulled, cut off and set to the side, and a pulling and twisting motion will continue until the candy is stretched along the table covered with a cotton tarp. Each cane or lollipop will be cut at a mark on the cotton. The length of the candy is determined by lines drawn on the table, but getting the same thickness every time takes years of practice. The cook will be pulling, twisting and cutting until the entire batch is gone. Depending on the size of the candy piece, cooks could be pulling thousands of times. On average, one batch will create over five hundred candy canes or over one thousand one-ounce lollipops.

The cane will be crooked by another employee from the packaging room and placed onto the conveyer belt that carries it to the packaging room. This process takes two people to make one cane.

The lollipops will get pulled the exact same way as the canes, but the diameter will change depending on the size of the lollipop. The lollipops will be twisted by another employee from the packaging room, and someone else will insert the stick. Usually two people will be enough for a normal lollipop, but if the spirals are being made, the cook and up to five others will be assisting, making it one of the most labor-intensive lollipops Hammond's makes. And instead of the stick being inserted into the candy, the candy is wrapped around the stick until it spirals all the way to the top. These lollipops resemble a unicorn horn.

For Christmas, the company makes a lollipop ornament, which is done exactly like a one-ounce lollipop except it has no stick. It is placed into a gift bag with a pretty red bow and a gold stretchy band to hang on a Christmas tree. These make fabulous gifts for guests at Christmas parties to "pick" from their host's tree and hang on theirs after a joyous Christmas dinner; they make an attractive and special gift decoration. The Christmas tree lollipop is also made using a Teflon mold for this shape, and a stick is inserted.

Valentine's Day calls for a heart-shaped lollipop, which is labor intensive, needing about five employees to assist the cook. A stainless steel triangle mold is used in this process as well as the lollipop stick. The shaper will form the lollipop into a round lollipop as usual, the stick will be inserted, and then it is put into the mold. A lollipop stick is placed on the top of the lollipop, and pressure is added as it pushes the candy into the mold; a triangle shape is formed at the bottom of the lollipop, while the stick forms the indent at the top of the heart. The workers accomplish all this in about fifteen to thirty seconds. These lollipops come in cinnamon, wild cherry and bubble gum flavors. All-natural flavors are also produced in the canes and the lollipops.

CANDY PULLER: A candy puller is used to pull, stretch and fold the candy upon itself, trapping air into the candy with every turn. This lightens the color of the candy and also the texture of the candy once it is solid.

CONSTRUCTION/BLOCKING TABLE: This is where the stripe jacket is built. "Blocks of candy" are formed and stretched by hand and placed next to each other, forming a stripe pattern. This jacket is wrapped around the center of the candy. Due to the open flame burning at the base of this table, it is very hot, and the cooks usually build for about twenty minutes. Old-fashioned handmade candy only has stripes on the outside, not through and through.

COOLING TABLE: Each table weighs almost three thousand pounds. Cold and room-temperature water circulates directly under the stainless steel top, cooling the candy from the bottom up. This is where the candy is poured and color, recycled candy and sometimes flavor are added.

CORN SYRUP TANK: This is the holding tank for the corn syrup, holding approximately 30,000 pounds. It is slightly warmed, and a valve allows the corn syrup to freely fill kettles and pots. A blue light will blink in the top of the tank to let the kitchen assistants know the level is running low. It is usually filled once a month. Hammond's does not use high-fructose corn syrup. On an average day at Hammond's, about 1,500 pounds of syrup is used. In addition to corn syrup, Hammond's now uses tapioca syrup.

FIRE MIXER: This is an open-fire candy stove with a kettle that mixes candy as it cooks. It is used for caramel, toffee, nougat, etc.

PILLOW MACHINE: This machine cuts many candies but primarily pillows. Other types of candies, including straws, jewels and the famous waffles, are all cut on this one machine. A simple adjustment as the candy is fed into the equipment determines the length of the candy. The width, or thickness, of the candy is determined by the cook and the way that the candy is being pulled. There are guides that help lead the candy into the right cutting die.

TEMPERING WHEEL: The tempering wheel helps distribute the cocoa butter in the chocolate. Tempered right, the cocoa butter crystals are contagious and affect the other cocoa butter, creating a uniform temper. The tempering wheel helps with that. Tempering is an artful process that takes time and an understanding of chocolate to learn. It is the melting, cooling and the distribution of cocoa butter (fat) crystals in the chocolate that creates the proper temper (shine, mouth feel and shelf life).

Notes

For the sake of brevity, citations from the *Denver Post* and *Rocky Mountain News* are abbreviated *DP* and *RMN*, respectively. Citations from these, as well as the periodicals *Municipal Facts* and the *Colorado Manufacturer and Consumer*, in the following notes were all obtained at the Denver Public Library, Western History Collection, and are marked DPLWHC.

Chapter 1

1. Goodstein, *North Side Story*, 193.
2. U.S. Bureau of the Census, Statistical Abstract of the United States, various issues; Population Division, www.census.gov/popest/index.html (accessed March 27, 2014).
3. Samuel H. Williamson, "Seven Ways to Compute the Relative Value of a U.S. Dollar Amount, 1774 to Present," MeasuringWorth, www.measuringworth.com/ppowerus, 2014.
4. *Town of Highlands: Its Progress, Prospects and Financial Condition: First Annual Report* (Highlands, CO: Highlands Chief Press, 1891), 10, quoted in Leonard and Noel, *Denver*, 61.
5. Pamela C. Whitenack, "Hershey, Milton Snavely, 1857–1945," Hershey Community Archives, www.hersheyarchives.org/resources (accessed May 19, 2014).

6. "Why Colorado-Made Candy Is Superior to the Product of Lower Altitudes," *Colorado Manufacturer and Consumer* 13 (July 1915): 4, DPLWHC.
7. *Candy and Ice Cream*, "Factory News" (March 1915): 29.
8. "Why Colorado-Made Candy Is Superior to the Product of Lower Altitudes," 4, DPLWHC.
9. Ibid.
10. *RMN*, "Denver to Have Big $500,000 Company," October 19, 1915, DPLWHC.
11. Ibid.
12. United States Department of Commerce, Bureau of the Census, *Historical Statistics of the United States, 1789–1945* (Washington, D.C.: U.S. Government Printing Office, 1949), 67.

Chapter 2

13. "A Zoo Is Born," www.denverzoo.org/about-us-history.
14. "Denver Auditorium Arena," Wikipedia (last modified June 12, 2014).
15. "Elitch Gardens History," www.elitchgardens.com.
16. Rykken Johnson, "Denver Candy Maker's Christmas Is at Hand," *DP*, May 4, 1977, DPLWHC.
17. *RMN*, "Business Conditions Good," September 5, 1920, DPLWHC.
18. Goodstein, *North Side Story*, 11.
19. Ibid., 42.
20. "Palette of Our Palates: A Brief History of Food Coloring and Its Regulation," *Comprehensive Reviews in Food Science and Food Safety* 8 (2009): 238, onlinelibrary.wiley.com.
21. *DP*, "Candy Man Arrested," September 5, 1920, DPLWHC.
22. *RMN*, "Candy Boards Reinstated in Stores," July 3, 1920, DPLWHC.
23. *Candy and Ice Cream*, "Factory News" (March 1915): 29.
24. "History," Great Western Sugar Cooperative, 2006, www.westernsugar.com/History.html.
25. *DP*, "Sugar Factories Will Slice Beets," September 19, 1920, DPLWHC.
26. Jake Friedman, "The Common Sense Candy Teacher," *Candy and Ice Cream* (March 1915): 5.
27. *Instructions for Starting a Candy Business* (Philadelphia: Candymakers Supply House, n.d.).

CHAPTER 3

28. Tolbert R. Ingram, ed., *The Yearbook of the State of Colorado* (n.p., 1926), 142, DPLWHC.
29. Ibid., 1928–29, 159.
30. Ibid., 1939–40, 120.
31. Clinton H. Scovell, "Counting Your Costs," *Candy and Ice Cream* (February 1915): 26.
32. "Barron's," Wikipedia (last modified May 27, 2014).
33. Goodstein, *North Side Story*, 214.
34. Johnson, "Denver Candy Maker's Christmas."
35. Sidney Redner, "Population History of Denver," physics.bu.edu/redner.
36. *Municipal Facts*, "Growth and Resources of Industrial Denver" (August 1920): 5, DPLWHC.
37. Ibid.
38. *Denver Times*, "Denver Proving Candy Center of Entire West," October 12, 1923, DPLWHC.
39. *DP*, "Lollipops Still Mainstay of Straser Candy Co Line," February 9, 1964, DPLWHC.

CHAPTER 4

40. Goodstein, *From Soup Lines to the Front Lines*, 228–34.
41. *RMN*, "Brecht and Nevin Candy Companies to Be One Operating Organization," March 10, 1931, DPLWHC.
42. *DP*, "Rocky Mountains Business Holding Above Last Year," September 23, 1934, DPLWHC.
43. *DP*, "Denver Chamber of Commerce Celebrates Fiftieth Anniversary," April 3, 1934, DPLWHC.
44. *DP*, "Denver Capital of U.S.," June 4, 1940, DPLWHC.
45. *DP*, "Carl Hammond, Founder and Owner of Company Dies," August 5, 1966, DPLWHC.

Chapter 5

46. *DP*, October 7, 1937, quoted in Leonard and Noel, *Denver*, 219.
47. *DP*, December 8, 1941, quoted in Leonard and Noel, *Denver*, 220.
48. "Candy Consumption and World War II," historyhodgepodge.com/2013/03/05/candy-consumption-wwii.
49. *DP*, "Cafes: Sugar Bowls to Go Off Thursday," February 2, 1942, DPLWHC.
50. "USS *Franklin*," Wikipedia (last modified on July 10, 2014).
51. *RMN*, "Ribbon Candy Like the Old Days," December 21, 1977, DPLWHC.
52. Robert Burns, "A Man's a Man for A' That" (1795), www.robertburns.org/works/496.shtm.
53. "One Hundred Years of Consumer Spending," U.S. Bureau of Labor Statistics, Consumer Expenditure Survey, 1950.

Chapter 6

54. *RMN*, "Ribbon Candy Like the Old Days."
55. Ibid.
56. Williamson, "Seven Ways to Compute the Relative Value of a U.S. Dollar Amount."
57. *RMN*, "Ribbon Candy Like the Old Days."
58. Ibid.
59. Ibid.
60. *DP*, "Hammond Estate Listed at $359,570," March 27, 1969, DPLWHC.
61. Johnson, "Denver Candy Maker's Christmas."
62. Ibid.

Chapter 8

63. *Merriam-Webster's Collegiate Dictionary*, 10th ed., s.v. "evolution."
64. Rebecca Landwehr, "Denver's Candy Kings," *Denver Business Journal* (December 12, 1999), www.bizjournals.com/denver/stories/1999/12/13/story3.html.

65. Ibid.
66. Ibid.
67. Ibid.
68. Ibid.
69. Aubrey Gordon, "Confection Connection Site Boosts Hammond's Candies' Sales," *Denver Business Journal* (November 24, 2002), www.bizjournals.com/denver/stories/2002/11/25/smallb.2.html.

Selected Bibliography

Goodstein, Phil. *From Soup Lines to the Front Lines: Denver during the Depression and World War II, 1927–1947*. Denver, CO: New Social Publications, 2007.

———. *North Side Story*. Denver, CO: New Social Publications, 2011.

Leonard, Stephen J., and Thomas J. Noel. *Denver: Mining Town to Metropolis*. Niwot: University Press of Colorado, 1990.

Index

About the Author

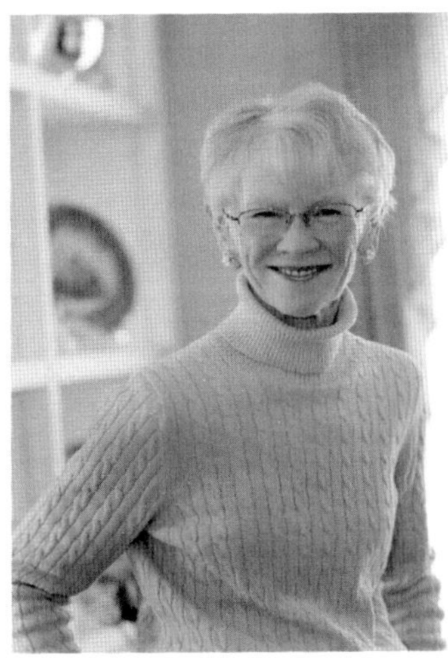

Laura Mahony Photography, Denver, Colorado.

Mary "Corky" Treacy Thompson recently embarked on her third career when she wrote her first book, *Of Rainbows in Puddles*, in 2013. A stay-at-home mom and professional volunteer actively involved for many years in PTA, scouting and the athletic and social activities of her daughter and two sons, she then followed a professional, paid path as the alumnae director of her alma mater, Manhattanville College, and as the executive director of the Westchester Association of Insurance and Financial Professionals. During that time, she actively served in the social justice ministries of the Immaculate Heart of Mary Church in Scarsdale, New York, and in 1993 was elected to the first of two terms on the board of education, of which she was also the president in 1997–98. In 2003, Corky and her husband, Greg, moved to Heritage Eagle Bend in Aurora, Colorado, where she continues her community involvement and is a member of the Society of St. Vincent de Paul at Our Lady of Loreto Catholic Church. She has been a mentor to incarcerated women in the Making Choices program at the Denver Women's Correctional Facility since 2006. In her leisure, Corky enjoys books, travel and the time she and her husband spend with their family, which now includes seven grandchildren in Colorado, Virginia and Connecticut. As a preteen, Corky aspired to be another Louisa May Alcott, holing up in her attic to write short stories on an orange crate, but she laughs at the realization that it took her sixty-plus years to complete her first book.